579/1980 $24.00

/50

Language and perception
in
Hegel and Wittgenstein

Language and perception
in
Hegel and Wittgenstein

David Lamb

St. Martin's Press
New York

ISBN 0-312-46612-9

Library of Congress Cataloging in Publication Data
Lamb, David.
    Language and perception in Hegel and Wittgenstein.
    Includes bibliographical references and index.
    1. Hegel, Georg Wilhelm Friedrich, 1770–1831.
    2. Wittgenstein, Ludwig, 1889–1951. 3. Languages - -
    Philosophy. 4. Perception. I. Title.
    B2949.L25L25   1980   193   80–505
    ISBN 0-312-46612-9

Contents

CHAPTER I.   LANGUAGE AND REALITY   1

1. The Wittgenstein moment   1
2. Hegel's criticism of sensory realism   3
3. Wittgenstein's conception of grammar   7
4. The nature convention dichotomy   11
5. Facts or rules?   16
6. Having a point   17
7. Agreement in 'form of life'   24
Notes   25

CHAPTER II.   GESTURES AND SOCIAL LIFE

1. Hegel and Wittgenstein on pointing and understanding   29
2. Is a form of life a way of life?   35
Notes   44

CHAPTER III.   PERCEPTION AND OBSERVATION IN HEGEL'S
                                        PHENOMENOLOGY   46

1. The fact-interpretation theory   46
2. Taking the standpoint of perception seriously   53
3. Critical realism   57
4. Summary   60
5. Sophisticated commonsense: the sophistry of 'insofar as'   61
6. Reason and observation in Hegel's *Phenomenology*   68
Notes   71

CHAPTER IV.   HEGEL'S CONCEPTION OF PHILOSOPHY   74

1. Hegel and the history of philosophy   74
2. The completion of human knowledge   83
3. The absolute   88
4. The difficulty with Hegel's *Phenomenology*   92
5. The unity of method and content: the preface to Hegel's
                                        Phenomenology   98
Notes   102

CHAPTER V.   HEGEL AND MODERN PHILOSOPHY   106

1. The critical element in description   106
2. Professional philosophy   115
3. The usefulness of Philosophy   120
4. The reality of philosophy   125
Notes   130

ABBREVIATIONS

References to the German editions of Hegel's work will be to *Werke* volumes I-XX, edited by E. Moldenhauer and K. M. Michel, Frankfurt am Main: Suhrkamp, 1970, hereafter indicated by the initials MM. As an additional guide each reference to the German text will be accompanied with a reference to the standard English text accompanied by the translators initial.

HEGEL

PG.   *The Phenomenology of Mind,* translated by J. Baillie, London: G. Allen and Unwin, 1949.

GP.   *Lectures on the History of Philosophy*, translated by E. S. Haldane and F. S. Simson, London: Routledge, 1955.

Enz.I. *The Logic of Hegel*, translated by W. Wallace, Oxford: University Press, 1873.

Enz.II. *Hegel's Philosophy of Nature,* translated by A. V. Miller, Oxford: University Press, 1970.

Enz.III. *Hegel's Philosophy of Mind*, translated by A. V. Miller, Oxford: University Press, 1970.

L.   *Hegel's Science of Logic*, translated by W. H. Johnson and L. G. Struthers, London: G. Allen & Unwin, 1929.

PR.   *Hegel's Philosophy of Right*, translated by T. M. Knox, Oxford: University Press, 1952.

WITTGENSTEIN

NB.   *Notebooks 1914-16*, edited by G. H. von Wright and G. E. M. Anscombe, Oxford: Blackwell, 1969.

TLP.   *Tractatus Logico-Philosophicus*, translated by D. F. Pears and B. F. McGuiness, London: Routledge, 1961.

RFM.   *Remarks on the Foundations of Mathematics*, edited by G. H. von Wright, R. Rhees, G. E. M. Anscombe, Oxford: Blackwell, 1967.

BB.   *The Blue and Brown Books,* Oxford: Blackwell, 1969.

PI. *Philosophical Investigations*, translated by G. E. M. Anscombe, Oxford: Blackwell, 1968.

OC. *On Certainty*, edited by G. E. M. Anscombe and G. H. von Wright, Oxford: Blackwell, 1969.

Z.   *Zettel,* edited by G. E. M. Anscombe and G. H. von Wright, Oxford: Blackwell, 1967.

LC. *Lectures and Conversations on Aesthetics, Psychology and Religious Belief*, edited by Cyril Barrett, Oxford: Blackwell, 1970.

ACKNOWLEDGEMENTS

I would like to express my thanks to the following: the editors
of *Clio* for permission to use some of the material included in
'Hegel and Wittgenstein on Language and Sense-Certainty', submitted
1978. Professor A. R. Manser for the use of unpublished papers
in the Department of Philosophy, University of Southampton.
Above all I wish to record my gratitude to Heather King without
whose secretarial skills and critical advice this book would not
have been published. The usual disclaimers apply.

David Lamb
1979

FOR   SUE

At any rate, with Hegel philosophy comes to an end. On the one
hand, because in his system he summed up its whole development
in its most splendid fashion; and on the other, because, even though
unconsciously, he showed us the way out of the labyrinth of systems
to real positive knowledge of the world.
                                         F. Engels

What is your aim in philosophy? - To show the way out of the fly-
bottle.
                                         L. Wittgenstein

Introduction

George Santayana was wrong when he said that 'those who have not studied the history of philosophy are compelled to re-enact its errors'. Many philosophers steeped in the history of their subject have failed to grasp that a standpoint, unique to them, is merely an old one fitted with new clothes. One might say that throughout the history of philosophy battles have been fought between combatants in virtual ignorance of the fact that only the battledress has changed. One of the underlying questions in this conflict has been: 'Is reality determined by human thought and language, or does it impose its form upon human thought and language?' Providing an answer to this question has usually involved an attempt to lay bare the foundations of human thought or language. In doing so philosophers have seen themselves conducting an inquiry into the structure of reality and of the cognitive faculties which stand in relation to nature's regularities. Occasionally, some philosophers have questioned this approach and have been at pains to initiate what they saw as a new and revolutionary conception of philosophy - even to the extent of describing their contribution as 'the end of philosophy'. In the nineteenth-century this claim was made by G. W. F. Hegel. In the twentieth-century it has been made by Ludwig Wittgenstein.

For many years it has been held that Wittgenstein's contribution to philosophy was a unique phenomenon, exploding into the Anglo-Saxon tradition with revolutionary ideas and a conception of philosophy unparalleled in the history of Western thought. It is now widely recognised that, far from being unique, Wittgenstein's philosophy is a contribution to a school of thought that can be traced back to Kant via Schopenhauer. To draw similarities between Wittgenstein's philosophy and German idealism is not as absurd as it might have seemed a few years earlier. Drawing attention to similarities between idealism and linguistic philosophy Raymond Plant cites the following anonymous remark in *The Times Literary Supplement*, July, 1969:

> ...reacting against Logical Atomism, the later Wittgenstein came up with many of the old idealist arguments in a new form. Hence the doubts cast upon the analytic-synthetic dichotomy, the corner stone of positivist thought.[1]

Apart from the substitution of the word 'language' for the idealist term 'mind' one could be forgiven for thinking that there has been little significant change brought about by the 'linguistic revolution'. But the thesis, recently proposed by Charles Taylor[2], that there is a close affinity between the later Wittgenstein and Hegel on language and

xi

sense-certainty has received surprisingly little attention. For, precisely because Wittgenstein was never a Hegelian, it would be an ironic note indeed if the linguistic revolution, through the later Wittgenstein, were to confirm the old Hegelian tradition. The considerable convergence of the later Wittgenstein, as commonly understood, and the Hegelian understanding of language thus deserves to be spelled out more fully. It is striking that the two philosophers argued very similarly against what might be called the empirical account of the relation between language and reality.

In Chapters I and II Wittgenstein's resolution of the dichotomy between language and reality will be considered. Wittgenstein will be presented against the background of Russell's logical atomism - a position which is combatted in the *Blue and Brown Books* and the *Philosophical Investigations*. It should be remembered, however, that Russell's sensory realism was a consequence of his 'liberation' from Hegelian idealism. Ironically it is the very standpoint of sensory realism that Hegel combats in the opening chapter of his first mature work, *The Phenomenology of Mind*. Similarities between Hegel and Wittgenstein's criticism of sensory realism will therefore be considered in both Chapters I and II. Following his discussion on sensory realism in the *Phenomenology*, Hegel turns to a dialogue with a 'perceiving consciousness' and raises several issues that bear more than a 'family resemblance' to Wittgenstein's remarks on perception in Part II of the *Philosophical Investigations*, thus forming the substance of the inquiry conducted in Chapter III. Whilst the first three chapters are critical of the empiricist division between language and reality, the final two chapters are primarily concerned with Hegel's attempt to transcend abstract distinctions drawn between philosophical discourse and reality. For both Hegel and Wittgenstein neither language and the world nor philosophical discourse and its object are externally related. In Chapter IV Hegel's conception of philosophy is outlined and his account of the unity of philosophical method with its object, absolute knowledge, is presented against the background of his historico-descriptive approach. In the final chapter the charges of conservatism, levelled at both Hegel and Wittgenstein are examined, and, in the context of a critique of professional philosophy, comparisons are drawn between Hegel and post-Wittgensteinian attitudes towards philosophy.

The purpose behind the following comparisons drawn between Wittgenstein and Hegel is not to show that the former was in any way influenced by Hegel but to reveal the extent to which the linguistic revolution, through the later Wittgenstein, has issued into and newly confirmed the old Hegelian or neo-Hegelian tradition against which it originally defined itself. And that is an irony of history which is indeed worthy of Hegel's attention.

David Lamb
1979

NOTES

[1] See R. Plant, *Hegel*, London: Allen & Unwin, 1973. p.187.

[2] Charles Taylor, 'The Opening Arguments of the *Phenomenology*', *Hegel*, edited by Alastair MacIntyre, New York: Doubleday, 1972.

I Language and reality

1. THE WITTGENSTEIN MOMENT

We now seem to have entered what might be called the
'Wittgenstein Moment' in philosophy. (J. Hartnack.)[1]

Is reality determined by consciousness or consciousness determined by
reality? Or is there an essential unity between them? From the
origins of philosophy in the Greek mind to the contemporary Wittgensteinian moment in philosophy these questions have been asked. Both
Hegel and Wittgenstein asserted the identity of thought and reality.
Whilst Hegel sought an ultimate reconciliation in the absolute Idea or
Spirit,Wittgenstein's resolution of the dichotomy between thought and
reality is expressed in the following remarks:

> Like everything else metaphysical the harmony between thought
> and reality is to be found in the grammar of the language.
> (Z.55)

> Grammar tells us what kind of object anything is. (PI.373)

To understand how these remarks express Wittgenstein's solution to
the above-mentioned problem it is necessary to understand what he
means by 'grammar' and 'objects'. How are objects determined by
grammar? Perhaps the best way to reach an understanding of these expressions is through a consideration of the views he rejected.

Both Hegel and Wittgenstein were critical of the empiricist account
of language and reality. The following passage can be considered as
typical of the form of empiricism which both repudiated:

> The meaning of an object-word can only be learned by hearing
> it frequently pronounced in the presence of the object. The
> association between word and object is just like any other
> habitual association, e.g. that between sight and touch. When
> the association has been established, the object suggests
> the word, and the word suggests the object...[2]

The underlying assumption here is that the meaning of a name must be
identical with the bearer of that name, which Wittgenstein attributes
to a tendency to 'sublime the logic of our language'. It is, he says,
a *queer* connection of a word with an object' caused by the philosopher's attempt to "bring out the relation between name and thing by

1

staring at an object in front of him and repeating a name or even the word 'this' innumerable times". (PI.38). To free the philosopher from this picture he points out that certain things can happen to the bearer of a name which need not happen to the name itself. The bearer of the name 'NN' may die but this does not imply that we cannot meaningfully use the name 'NN' again. Wittgenstein's point (PI.38-43) is that the meaning of a name is determined by the rules of usage, not by the thing it refers to. A name can still have meaning even when the object referred to no longer exists.

A few years earlier, in the *Blue and Brown Books*, Wittgenstein drew attention to the same theme, warning against the "temptation to look about you for some object which you might call 'the meaning'" (BB.1). This temptation, he claimed, arises from the tendency to look for a corresponding substance behind every substantive (BB.1). Combatting this tendency Wittgenstein set out to undermine two concepts of meaning. The first is an objective account, according to which the meaning of a word is an object or thing correlated to the word, and the second is a subjective or psychological approach, according to which the meaning is equated with an inner *Bild*, a view which is countered in his refutation of solipsism and his famous denial of the possibility of a private language.[3] Both accounts, however, share the assumption that the foundation of language is to be found in the activity of naming; one is alleged to either name objects or mental images.

In his later works Wittgenstein combats the assumptions of sensory realism with the advice to look at the actual usage of words. A word has its meaning by virtue of its role in human practices. This does not mean, as several philosophers have thought, that Wittgenstein simply substitutes the traditional 'objects' of philosophy with the formalistic rules of language and syntax. When he asks us not to think, not to look for an underlying realm of meaning, but to look at the 'language games' within which the words are used, he is calling into account the whole business of reaching conclusions about language and reality in an abstract manner. In doing so he is casting doubt upon the credibility of philosophy as a science which determines the fixed structure of reality. Wittgenstein's emphasis upon use matches the Hegelian stress on the fluidity of concepts. For Wittgenstein, as with Hegel, the area of interest is what we do with language rather than what it is. The significance of the later Wittgenstein's stress on the social basis of language invites comparison with Hegel, who likewise began his first mature work, the *Phenomenology*, with a criticism of the empiricist account of language and certainty.

2. HEGEL'S CRITICISM OF SENSORY REALISM

> Both in the sphere of the social order (*Sittlichkeit*) where
> language embodies laws and commands, and in the sphere of
> actual life, where it appears as conveying advice, the con-
> tent of what it expresses is the essential reality, and
> language is the form of that essential content.
> (PG.MM.376/B.530)

Like Wittgenstein, Hegel combatted sensory realism in both its objective
and subjective guises, rejecting both realism and solipsism. At the
outset of the *Phenomenology* Hegel presents a phenomenological account
of the difficulties facing the philosopher who embraces a sensory
realist account of the foundations of language. Parallels with the
opening sections of Wittgenstein's *Investigations* are striking. In both
cases attention is focussed upon difficulties in the philosopher's
belief that one can make a foundational act of referring. Depicting the
standpoint of sensory realism Hegel seizes upon the terms 'here', 'now'
and 'this', which, on a Russellian theory of language, stand as logically proper names. As with Wittgenstein, the model of ostensive definition is revealed as an inadequate account of the primary connection
between word and thing. Both Wittgenstein and Hegel agree that any
meaningful reference takes place within a wider system of conventions,
rules and social practices. Hegel's treatment of sensory realism is,
like Wittgenstein's, presented in terms of two moments; an objective and
subjective account. In the objective moment Hegel considers a consciousness which places emphasis upon the passive experience of the
object. But, in the absence of any understanding of the rules which
govern a meaningful act of referring, it proves impossible for the sensory realist to indicate which object is meant. Hegel depicts him
pointing to a tree and then to a house in an attempt to make a foundational reference to the immediate 'here' of his experience. Lacking
a more sophisticated set of concepts the sensory realist cannot make a
foundational reference.

> The Here is, for example, the tree. I turn about and this
> truth has disappeared and has changed into its opposite: the
> Here is not a tree, but a house. The Here itself does not
> disappear; it *is* and remains in the disappearance of the
> house, tree, and so on, and is indifferently house, tree.
> The This is shown once again to be *mediated simplicity*, in
> other words, to be *universality*. (PG.MM.85/B.152-3).

Now most people would have no difficulty in distinguishing a house
from a tree in their field of vision. But most people are not in the
position which philosophers like Russell have ascribed to them.

Hegel's remarks are directed at the philosophical assumption that one's initial knowledge of houses and trees, and other objects in the physical world, is acquired primarily through an act of ostensive definition unmediated by cultural factors. Hegel's remarks about the difficulty of making a unique reference to a tree have a decidedly modern ring. Consider, for example, what the contemporary taxonomist, G. G. Simpson, has to say about immediate individuation, when formulating principles for the classification of elements within the natural world.

> If each of the many things in the world were taken as distinct, unique, a thing in itself unrelated to any other thing, perception of the world would disintegrate into complete meaninglessness. That would be true if each thing, say for instance each tree, were considered as a wholly separate individual; of course, it would not then *be* a tree, for 'tree' is a collective concept not applicable to a single object considered without relationship to any other. It could indeed be argued...that even the individual tree could not be perceived as a thing in itself, for each of the sensory perceptions is meaningful only as a collective generalisation, and without some form of ordering and abstraction the tree would disintegrate into a formless mosaic of 'green' (distinct from the sensations derived from any other green tree) 'rough feeling', 'branching', and so on. [4]

'There could be no intelligible language', concludes Simpson, 'if each thing (or each perception) were designated by a separate word, and no rational thought if symbols did not generalise characteristics and relationships shared by innumerable different objects'. [5] This is Hegel's point: in the absence of universality there can be no significant account of experience.

> If nothing else is said of a thing except that it is an actual thing, an external object, this only makes it the most universal of all possible things, and thereby we express its likeness, its identity, with everything, rather than its difference from everything else. When I say 'an individual thing', I at once state it to be really quite a universal, for everything is an individual thing: and in the same way 'this thing' is everything and anything we like.
> (PG.MM.92/B.160)

Hegel's point is that the mere recording of a datum of sense-experience cannot serve as an adequate reference since something that is not given in sensory experience is necessary. The sensory realist,

invited by Hegel to write down the word 'now' to designate the time of
his experience, cannot explain whether his 'now' refers to noon-time,
night-time, or when. The 'now', says Hegel, 'is determined through
and *by means* of the fact that something else, namely day and night, is
not' (PG.MM.84/B.152). Similar problems occur in the attempt to make
a foundational spatial reference. The sensory realist who tries to
indicate an ultimate 'here' of immediate experience cannot do so unless he is prepared to make a reference to above or below, to the
right of or to the left. And giving references presupposes some
definite knowledge. One can only give a direction to the Town Hall if
one has some knowledge of other buildings or streets by means of which
the Town Hall can be located. A precise location of an object can
only be given if there are other objects whose location is beyond dispute. These objects must be capable of being located by the same
process, for there are no ultimate 'heres'. Every reference, says
Hegel, is an implied comparison, a view which has been wrongly interpreted by Russell as a denial of the possibility of unique reference
since it would seem that every reference is to the whole. Says
Russell:

> The view of Hegel...is that the character of any portion
> of the universe is so profoundly affected by its relations
> to other parts and to the whole, that no true statement
> can be made about any part except to assign it its place
> in the whole. Since its place in the whole depends upon
> all the other parts, a true statement about its place in
> the whole will at the same time assign the place of every
> other part in the whole.[6]

Russell, of course, shares the sensory realist assumption that the
only alternative to limitless holism is a foundational reference.
Captivated by the 'proper name theory of words' he interprets the
Hegelian rejection of foundational meanings as a denial that words
can have any meaning at all. Thus:

> "The word 'John' means all that is true of John." But as a
> definition this is circular, since the word 'John' occurs
> in the defining phrase. In fact, if Hegel were right, no
> word could begin to have a meaning, since we should need
> to know already the meanings of other words in order to state
> at all the properties of what the word designates...[7]

It is with uncanny accuracy that Russell approaches the defects in
his own position, for Hegel's trump card is that if words did have
meanings of the kind that Russell believes in, then, in the absence
of any definite system of rules, it would be impossible to make any

5

reliable and unambiguous reference to them. But whilst Hegel maintains that every reference presupposes co-ordinates it does not follow that every reference presupposes equally necessary co-ordinates. That co-ordinates are necessary for a meaningful reference to be made does not specify how many and what co-ordinates there should be. When I refer to the knife by saying that it is to the left of the salt, it is necessary that I refer to a co-ordinate but it is not necessarily the salt and not something else. The 'cold Winter of 1972' might work as a co-ordinate for locating the time of my grandfather's death but one can refer to the event by some other co-ordinate as required. Merely because we need co-ordinates to make a meaningful reference does not commit us to an unlimited holism of Marshall Smuts' dimensions.

One of the problems with the position Hegel depicts as sensory realism is its lack of a criterion of sameness. In the absence of a shared system of practices, a universal, how can one be said to be experiencing the same sensory experience on different occasions? How does the realist know that his application of names to sensations is consistent? Suppose that Hegel's sensory realist decides to employ the term 'tree' as a name of his sensation of the tree standing in his visual space. What is it, asks Hegel, that guarantees that his use of the term in the future will have any meaning? Commenting on Wittgenstein's remarks on sameness and identity (PI.215), Peter Winch develops Wittgenstein's thought along lines that are very close to Hegel when he says:

> It is only in terms of a given *rule* that we can attach a specific sense to the words 'the same'. In terms of the rule governing the use of the word 'mountain', a man who uses it to refer to Mount Everest on one occasion and to Mont Blanc on another occasion is using it in the same way each time; but someone who refers to Mont Blanc as 'Everest' would not be said to be using this word in the same way as someone who used it to refer to Mount Everest. So the question: 'What is it for a word to have meaning? leads on to the question: What is it for someone to follow a rule?...Suppose that the word 'Everest' has just been ostensively defined to me. It might be thought that I could settle at the outset what is to count as the correct use of this word in the future by making a conscious decision to the effect: 'I will use this word only to refer to *this* mountain'. And that of course, in the context of the language which we all speak and understand, is perfectly intelligible. But, just because it presupposes the settled institution of the language we all speak and understand, this does not throw any light on

the philosophical difficulty. Obviously we are not permitted to presuppose that whose very possibility we are investigating. It is just as difficult to give any account of what is meant by 'acting in accordance with my decision' as it is to give an account of what it was to 'act in accordance with the ostensive definition' in the first place. However emphatically I point at this mountain here before me and however emphatically I utter the words 'this mountain', my decision still has to be *applied* in the future, and it is precisely what is involved in such an application that is here in question.[8]

It is in the light of Wittgenstein's illuminating account of what is involved in 'following a rule' that one can begin to appreciate Hegel's own treatment of sensory realism. Both Hegel and Wittgenstein maintained that one cannot isolate a particular 'this' of sensation and present it as one of the foundations of language and thought. In the absence of a framework of rules the very attempt to isolate and refer to an ultimate particular of sensation causes it to evaporate into everything. It is necessary to bring in something else. Hegel, for his part, emphasised the epistemological primacy of the concrete universal whilst Wittgenstein emphasised the primacy of grammar over the objects of sense.

3. WITTGENSTEIN'S CONCEPTION OF GRAMMAR

> The spirit comes to guide me in my need,
> I write, 'In the beginning was the deed'.
> [Goethe, *Faust*]

Referring to Wittgenstein's later philosophy, E. K. Specht points out that:

There is, therefore, no third sphere, additional to language and objects, a sphere of meaning that lends life to the whole of language. Rather, language wins its sense and function in Wittgenstein simply from the practice of people, from their action with linguistic signs and objects. Thus, for Wittgenstein semantic analysis amounts to analysis of actual linguistic use and the analysis of its place in human activities. The only approach to the meaning of a word consists in studying the ways it is used in the concrete *language games* of our language. In this sense, Wittgenstein repeatedly says: 'Let the use of words teach you their meaning'.[9]

It is clear that for Wittgenstein, analysis is not the analysis of the ultimate particles of sense-content but of the grammar of social activity in which a reference to any sense content has significance. An objection to this approach, from the standpoint of sensory realism, might go as follows: 'although the analysis of the grammar of a word affords access to the structure of the object signified, the correctness of the grammatical analysis does not ultimately depend on languag but rather on the structure of the object signified, and only from tha source can it derive its justification. In this way the primacy of th grammatical analysis, demanded by Wittgenstein, became questionable and had to be replaced by the priority of the ontological mode of observation'.[10]

Now this objection, says Specht, 'operates from the beginning on the basis of the atomic model of language; it is tacitly assumed that the objects are there previous to language, that the language is subsequently added and that the rules of linguistic usage are read off from the objects. Only in this way is it at all possible to found an investigation into the structure of objects'.[11] But if the rules of usage are not read off from the objects, as Specht and Wittgenstein insist, to what extent is the object relevant, and to what extent is it determined by grammar?

In spite of his demand that philosophy should in no way interfere with the actual use of language, (PI.124) Wittgenstein uses his key concept of 'grammar' in a way that does not accord with normal linguistic usage. The above-mentioned advice, however, does not apply to Wittgenstein's own terminological inventiveness - or to anyone else's - but only to attempts to draw up a system of signs intended to replace or render a more accurate account of things than ordinary language or the language of the sciences, such as the programme indicated in the *Tractatus*. Wittgenstein's grammar is not the grammar of the grammarians with its emphasis on phonetics, accidence and syntax, which investigates language with regard to what is spoken. This phonetical grammar in both Wittgenstein and Hegel's eyes, would be a formless grammar of material only, since it is primarily concerned with the empirical study of the material of linguistic signs.[12] By w of contrast Wittgenstein's conception of grammar is that of a grammar of meaning, describing the rules which govern the actual use of the sign, and its applicability within a given context.[13] It is in this sense that Wittgenstein calls reflections about linguistic usage 'grammatical investigations'. (PI.90) or 'grammatical notes'. (PI.232 and 'grammatical remarks'. (PI.574).

Sometimes Wittgenstein speaks of a tendency to confuse 'surface grammar' with 'depth grammar'. (PI.664) In this respect surface grammar would correspond to the rules for the use of a word, in the way it is used in the construction of a sentence, whilst depth gramma refers to those rules of usage that do not immediately reveal themselves on the 'superficial form of our grammar'. (RFM.1.108) An understanding of the relationship between depth and surface grammar is crucial to an understanding of Wittgenstein's later conception of philosophical analysis. According to Wittgenstein certain philosophical problems were bound up with the tendency to confuse one kind of expression with another. For example, when speaking of philosophical puzzlement in the *Blue Book* he refers to St. Augustine's problem concerning the measurement of time. (BB.26) The problem for Augustine was, 'How can we measure time, since the past is gone and the future has yet to come?' Augustine, says Wittgenstein, was puzzled over the different grammars concerning the word 'measure': that of measuring time and that of measuring two marks on a travelling band. Wittgenstein depicts this confusion as being typical of philosophical confusion, which, he claims, is due to the 'fascination which the analogy between two similar structures in our language can exert on us'. (BB.26) In order to combat this fascination he employs a 'grammatical' mode of analysis. In the *Investigations* he says:

> Our investigation is therefore a grammatical one. Such an investigation sheds light on our problem by clearing misunderstandings away. Misunderstandings concerning the use of words, caused, among other things, by certain analogies between the forms of expression in different regions of language. - Some of them can be removed by substituting one form of expression for another; this may be called an 'analysis' of our forms of expression, for the process is something like one of taking a thing apart. (PI.90)

In order to understand how Wittgenstein's conception of grammar gives us the determination of objects we must turn to a further development of this line of reasoning: the 'grammatical proposition'. Consider the difference between the following pair of propositions:

a. Every rod in the store has a price tag.
b. Every rod in the store has a length.

Their resemblance is superficial and confined to surface grammar only. An analysis of their depth grammar reveals a clear distinction between the two propositions. The first proposition is a straightforward empirical statement referring to certain objects in the store, which can be verified as true or false. But the second proposition is different: what would it be like for it to be false? What would count as an example of mistakenly thinking that all the rods had a length - as opposed to mistakenly thinking that all the rods were of the same length? Proposition (b) is not completely nonsensical; it is not without a referent in the way that 'Round Monday sleeps with Tuesday' lacks a conceivable referent. Proposition (b) refers to actual rods which can be handled and are located in the store. It is, however, infallibly true, even trivially true. It says nothing more than proposition (a), although it says even less since it does not give us any information about the price tags. If I know that there are rods in the store, and I know what rods are, then I must also know that they have a length. The expression 'and they have a length' is superfluous In this sense proposition (b) is without content. But whilst it is trivial it does make a reference that other propositions do not: it draws our attention to the grammatical rules for the usage of the word 'rods' and 'length'. And insofar as it is trivially true or its negation absurdly false, its truth or falsity does not depend on the objec referred to, but on the rules of usage governing the conventions by which a linguistic sign signifies an object. One utters the proposition 'Every rod has a length' to point out that the rules for the correct usage of the term 'rod' exclude the possibility of the term 'rod' being applied to phenomena not having a length. For this reason proposition (b) is what Wittgenstein would call a grammatical proposition. Grammatical propositions express rules; they show what it makes sense to say on a given occasion. Throughout his later works Wittgenstein offers several examples of grammatical propositions; for example, 'My images are private', (PI.251) 'Only I myself can know whether I am feeling pain', (PI.253) 'This body has extension', (PI.252 'Machines cannot think', (PI.360) and 'White is lighter than black'. (RFM.1.104)

Grammatical propositions therefore make an additional reference that ordinary propositions do not make; they refer to the rules of meaning governing the expressions occurring in them. Whereas ordinary propositions can be falsified by an appeal to the objects of sense, grammatical propositions are unaffected. A claim to have observed a rod having no length would not be accepted as an account of a genuine observation. One may observe something having no length but whatever it was could not be a rod. The only possibility of the proposition 'Every rod has a length' being falsified would be a change in the grammatical rules for the usage of the terms 'rod' and 'length'. Whether such a change is possible would depend upon the type of activities which require a distinction between rods with length and those without length, which would probably involve an activity in which some gaseous medium was signified by the term 'rod' together with the appropriate criterion for determining what might be called its length.

Similar considerations might apply to other grammatical propositions If the proposition 'machines can think' were to become acceptable, a dramatic change in the grammar of 'machines' and 'think' would be necessary. And this would involve a change in attitude as well as fact. The line between analytic and synthetic is not as strong as som philosophers have thought. To be sure the kind of social change necessary to effect such a change of attitudes would be enormous, but not beyond the limits of human adaptability. Moreover, it would not be merely a matter of humans deciding to change their attitudes. The machines would have to do most of the convincing, and not necessarily by rational argument, since 'one does not argue with machines, one switches them off'. If such a change were to come about it would probably parallel the events which forced the white races to accept the fact that Red Indians and negroes were human beings capable of thoughts and feelings.[14] It would involve a redefinition of the concept of a 'human being'. So with sufficient protest it is conceivable that machines, like 'other races', could effect a change in the grammatical rules governing 'machines' and 'think'. It is worth noting that less than half a century ago 'The poorer classes are without intelligence' was a grammatical proposition of the kind that we have been discussing.

But, one might object, no matter how we change the rules of usage, a grammatical proposition makes a reference to certain objects. How independent are the rules of usage from the objects signified? According to the above argument it would follow that the significance of a grammatical proposition is determined not by the structure of the object to which it refers, but by the consistency of the rules of usage to which it also refers. The issue we have touched upon is the nature-convention dichotomy. Is language determined by the natural facts or by the rules and conventions?

4. THE NATURE-CONVENTION DICHOTOMY

'We decide *spontaneously*' (I should like to say) 'on a new language game.' [Wittgenstein, RFM.III.23]

The nature-convention dichotomy would constitute, for Hegel, a distinction created by the 'abstract understanding'. The truth of each claim would be grasped in a further stage of development, which would involve a recognition of the internal unity between the linguistic signs and the method of classifying the phenomena signified by them. According to Specht, Wittgenstein avoids the one-sided abstractions of the nature-convention dichotomy when he 'circumvents these false emphases by building on the *simultaneity* of the *introduction of linguistic signs and organization into classes*'.[15] On this line of reasoning facts do not serve as the foundations of language any more than language serves as the foundation of our knowledge of reality. Instead language is seen as an activity one engages in when working upon the natural world, imposing form on it, meeting its resistance, and so on. The natural world is presented to us as a series of facts, classified into various species and types. This cannot be denied. But this classification is undertaken and acquired in learning the language,

11

an activity which is inseparable from learning how to live in the world.

It is easy to read into the above rejection of a realist ontology a considerable resemblance to the conventionalist and pragmatic theories of C. I. Lewis. And, as we shall see, Wittgenstein tends to give an exaggerated account of the moment of conventionalism whenever he confronts the realist perspective. The conventionalist approach, favoured by Lewis, was known as 'conceptual pragmatism'. According to Lewis the human spirit, freely and spontaneously, draws up the *a priori* structures for its understanding of reality, and holds on to them for no other reason than their pragmatic utility. These structures, he claimed, are not capable of being refuted by experience because they make experience possible in the first place.

> It is given experience, brute facts, the *a posteriori* element in knowledge which the mind accepts willy-nilly. The *a priori* represents an attitude in some sense freely taken, a stipulation of the mind itself, and a stipulation which might be made in some way other if it suited our bent or need...Mind contributes to experience the element of order, of classification, categories and definition. Without such, experience would be unintelligible. Our knowledge of the validity of these is simply consciousness of our own fundamental ways of acting and our own intellectual intent. Without this element knowledge is impossible, and it is here that whatever truths are necessary and independent of experience must be found.16

Wittgenstein holds a similar view to Lewis with regard to the necessity of *a priori* propositions. But this view depends to a large extent on the assumption of the free activity of human beings in the drawing up of language games. For instance, if we reject the realist assumption that facts and the rules of language are read off from reality and accept that they are presented within the various language games according to grammatical rules, what are we then to say concerning the creation of language games? Are they freely and spontaneously drawn up? If not, what is the nature of the restraints? Wittgenstein (PI.355 and RFM.111.23) encourages the conventionalist interpretation of the relationship between language games and reality.17 And in a paper concerned with Wittgenstein's conception of necessity M. Dummett interprets Wittgenstein as a 'full-blooded conventionalist'.

> Wittgenstein goes in for full-blooded conventionalism; for him the logical necessity of any statement is always the *direct* expression of a linguistic convention. That a given statement is necessary consists always in our having expressly decided to treat that very statement as unassailable;

it cannot rest on our having adopted certain other conventions which are found to involve our treating it so.[18]

To understand where Wittgenstein stood on the problem of conventionalism it is necessary to refer to *Moore's Lecture Notes*, where it is argued that in one sense grammatical rules are conventional but in another sense they are not. Here he seems to be saying that a grammatical rule is conventional in the sense that we are free to adopt a new one, but they are not conventional in the sense that once one is adopted it must be applied consistently, or, if not, another must be adopted and applied consistently. Thus:

If a word is to have significance, we must commit ourselves ...There is no use in correlating noises to facts, unless we commit ourselves to using the noise in a particular way again - unless the correlation has consequences.[19]

An important factor in the drawing up of a new language game is therefore consistency. One might say that when William Webb-Ellis picked up the ball and ran with it, his action would have been seen only as an infringement of the rules of soccer if he had not gone on to apply the rules of the new game consistently.

But what are the limits to this spontaneity? Consistency is undoubtedly important, but on the other hand, it does not seem to be enough. It is extremely unlikely, for example, that one could create a new game by picking up the ball and eating it, even if one were prepared to follow this rule consistently. Imagine a latter-day Webb-Ellis attempting such a radical departure from the rules of modern soccer. Such a break with conventions was only possible because the rules and institutions governing the game of soccer in those days were more informal. In a very important sense William Webb-Ellis helped to create the rules of soccer as well as rugby. The point is that we do not enter this world and freely set up any convention that comes to mind. We are born into a world in which grammatical rules are established in the language and way of life. Only in the sense that they do not interfere with too many existing rules are we free to create a new set of conventions. But if they do interfere with existing conventions the new must either replace the old or be rejected completely.

In his later works, Wittgenstein was committed to working out a solution whereby the rules for the use of an expression are partly arbitrary and partly non-arbitrary. The central problem is 'Why can't anything count as a rule?' And what are the limiting factors? In the *Remarks on the Foundations of Mathematics* he considers an example where the moment of arbitrariness is in the foreground. He points out that the proposition '12 inches = 1 foot' is said to express a convention. (RFM.V.1-2) This is arbitrary in the sense that there is no reason why 12 inches should be a foot. We could use other symbols, for example, '24 inches = 1 foot'. But in a very important sense we are prevented from changing this convention, since many other things would have to change. As Wittgenstein says, 'it is grounded in a technique'. (RFM.V.1) In this way the linear measuring game of feet and inches is partly arbitrary and partly non-arbitrary.

With colour words the moment of arbitrariness is greater. We can and do draw up different conventions for the application of colour words providing that they do not clash with too many other well-established conventions. Should this be doubted one might consider the way in which the colour spectrum is classified differently in other societies. In Russian, the terms '*goluboj*' (light blue) and '*sinij*' (dark blue) have only the fact that they are colours in common, which suggests that in Russian one might be prohibited from saying that a table, which is (in English) a mixture of light and dark blue, is blue all over. The Eskimoes, as everyone knows, employ several words to refer to what the English refer to as snow, largely because it makes sense to distinguish between several different substances which have different functions for them. Assuming there was a society having no use for the motor car, they might find it equally puzzling to discover scores of names, such as 'Cortina', 'Victor' and 'Avenger' for similar pieces of machinery. For similar reasons a distinction is made in the Phillipines between what can only be described as wet and dry colours. These examples serve as an indication that language, culture and livelihood conditions and determines our experience of the natural world.

Nevertheless, there are certain limits to the arbitrariness of the grammatical rules for the usage of colour words. But the extent to which these limitations are imposed by the natural facts is not as clear as many philosophers imply. Consider, for example, the kind of thing philosophers have in mind when they utter the statement 'Red and blue cannot occur simultaneously in the same visual field'. According to F. Ferre[20] this statement is true and linguistically necessary because of the linguistic rules, though it is contingent in another sense because its truth is dependent upon certain 'facts of nature'. These 'facts of nature' could well be the:

> facts of physics (the production and absorption of energy
> in the form of light waves) and the facts of biology (the
> equipment of language using animals with sight). This is
> a dependance not on the particular *propositions* only, which
> is made true analytically by the rules of the colour *language
> game*; but it is a dependance of the *language game* itself
> on facts of human experience, interests, and purposes within
> the natural order as we find it.[21]

14

Ferre concludes that the 'incompatibility of colours may justifiably be held to be both a necessary and - in a more profound sense - a contingent truth. What is necessary in a language game may not be necessary as a language game'.[22]

The explanation of synthetic *a priori* propositions, on this account, is that the statement 'Red and blue cannot occur simultaneously in the same visual field' is necessary *a priori* but contingently synthetic because the language game might not have existed. But one of the problems here is that Ferre speaks as if the facts are somehow external to the language game whose contingency rests upon them. In the case of the language game of colour incompatibility the moment of contingency arises over 'certain facts of nature' such as the possibility of universal blindness. It is true that if such a state existed we would probably have no use for statements asserting the incompatibility of colours. But what is not clear is whether this would be a limit imposed by the natural fact of universal blindness. If universal blindness were such that it would not make sense to speak of colour incompatibility at all, then it would not make sense to speak of the 'fact' of universal blindness. It is true that if some affliction rendered the entire human population blind overnight the language game of colour incompatibility could still be played, but the conditions necessary for there to be no such game at all would be a state of blindness such that there would have never been any point in playing it. This would entail a human population that had never referred to activities bound up with seeing colours at any point in their history. Consequently there would be no sighted persons, and for this reason, it would make no sense at all to speak of the fact of universal blindness, since there would be no record of anyone seeing. There could only be a point in recording universal blindness as a fact if someone claims to be able to do certain things which others could not do. If universal blindness had been a feature of the human race from the beginning there would be no point in speaking about universal blindness. We can only have facts if there is a point in stating them. As soon as one speaks of a fact he presupposes a language game in which it has sense. For this reason we cannot speak of the contingency of the fact of universal blindness since if it were the case there would be no language game in which it could be stated.

The problem with Ferre's position is that he has placed certain facts outside the various language games. In this way he has sought to limit the spontaneity in the drawing up of a language game to certain natural foundations. But against this view it is necessary to point out that what counts as a basic fact, or a foundation, can only be so if it has a point in a language game.

5. FACTS OR RULES?

> How do I know that this colour is red? - It would be an answer
> to say: "I have learnt English". [Wittgenstein, PI.381]

Commenting on the necessity of Wittgenstein's language games Specht
says:

> Summing up what has been said so far, the general picture of
> the relationship between arbitrariness and non-arbitrariness
> in the drawing up of a language game is as follows: our
> language games are *arbitrary* insofar as the rules constituting
> them, although drawn up in the closest connection with certain
> facts of nature, do not result from the facts *by necessity*.[23]

This approach exhibits the kind of honest compromise that might appeal
to Wittgenstein's English followers, and there is an important sense in
which language games are drawn up in connection with certain facts of
nature, but on a closer examination certain problems begin to appear.
In the first phase of the argument the move is made away from the assertion that language is read off from the facts. Specht is faithful to
Wittgenstein at this stage. To make this move it is necessary to show
that what counts as a fact can only be meaningful within the context of
a grammar. However, when faced with the possibility of unlimited
spontaneity in drawing up the rules of grammar, there is nothing to
fall back on but an appeal to the resistance of the natural facts,
which, it has been argued, can only be asserted within the context of
a language game. There seems to be no point within this circle for
facts to be admitted unless they already count as facts in some existing language game. This suggests that the limitations to spontaneity
in the drawing up of a language game must lie elsewhere.[24] Of course
the facts do impose certain limitations. This is not disputed. What
is disputed is the view that the facts play an ultimate, or foundationa
role in the determination of a language game. In fairness to Specht
however, it must be acknowledged that he recognised that language games
'do not result from the facts by necessity'.

To resolve this problem let us consider, again, the example of colour
words where the moment of arbitrariness was said to be greater. It was
argued that if the human race were sightless there would be no use for
the concept 'red'. But it is not the physiological fact of sightless-
ness that limits the rules of usage for the application of the concept
'red', but the point of having the concept 'red'. If the human race
had always been sightless we would have no point in stating this as a
fact. If someone ever claimed to possess the faculty of sight, it is
possible that his utterances would be treated as evidence of a new kind
of madness, or physical maladjustment, as in H. G. Wells's *The Kingdom
of the Blind*.

Only if the point of playing the language game of colour words were lost would we lose the concept 'red'.[25] But from where does the point come? And the answer is: from our activities, from human practices, human desires. If this is so there is no natural world existing independently of our ways of taking hold of it. What is given as natural appears to us from within our historic standpoint, culture, rules and training. The natural world is what is presented as natural from within one's form of life. The Eskimos' several words for what the English call 'snow' is not determined by the natural facts but by the point of having several words for the phenomena. And this point is determined according to the social composition of their society, their methods of work, transport, trade, and so on. It is bound up with the sort of things they do with the snow, and their reasons for classifying snow into various types.

6. HAVING A POINT

> The game, one would like to say, has not only rules but also a *point* [Wittgenstein, PI.564]

Having a point means having a relevance, a significance, in our lives. Specht describes it as a 'salient point, decisive moment, purpose, sense'.[26] He interprets Wittgenstein's remarks in PI.62 and RFM.II.71 and II.75, as an implication that 'our ordinary language-games would lose their purpose and sense if the facts of nature were different'.[27] What is the force of the term 'would' here? Is it not the case that societies persist with certain linguistic rules and conventions long after the most profound changes in the objects and institutions to which they refer? If the facts were to change it is possible that many of our ordinary language games would go on as before.

Now it is true that Wittgenstein says that "calculating would lose its point if *confusion* supervened. Just as the use of words 'green' and 'blue' would lose its point". (RFM.II.75) But so would the term 'confusion'. It is not that our ability to calculate and to use the terms 'green' and 'blue', guarantees that there is no confusion, but that we do calculate and so on means that our attitudes are set against confusion. This is why he says that 'The concept of calculating excludes *confusion*'. (RFM.II.75) So Wittgenstein does not argue here, at least, that 'ordinary language games would lose their point if the facts of nature were different'. On the contrary, he is saying that because we have adopted a certain language game, and are prepared to adhere to it, we have determined (in the case of calculating, for example) what is to count as confusion: the practice of calculating determines what is to count as a confusion in mathematics.

One of the consequences of adopting Specht's interpretation is that once we accept the natural facts as constitutive of the limits to spontaneity the criticism of Wittgenstein's tendency to over-emphasise the moment of conventionalism centres only on the factual limitations to his 'imaginary' language games and anthropological examples. To do so is to reveal a commitment to a realist ontology. But this is to forget that the rejection of a realist ontology means that human practice becomes the guide for suggestions concerning conceptual reform. For this reason it is more rewarding to locate the shortcomings of the alternative language games presented by Wittgenstein in their social and political consequences.

In the *Remarks on the Foundations of Mathematics* Wittgenstein presents the following example:

> As we could imagine people of a tribe who, when they dropped coins on the ground, did not think it worth their while to pick them up. (They have, say, an idiom for these occasions: 'It belongs to the others' or the like...) (RFM.V.8)

One might wonder what sort of an economy this tribe have. Presumably these coins have little exchange value, or perhaps they suffer from hyper-inflation on the Weimar scale in which case the currency is not wo bothering to pick up. Yet the parenthetical remark rules out hyper-inflation since it conceives of a convention which maintains that the ownership of money changes the moment it hits the ground. Now such a set of conventions might be employed by the proverbial 'eccentric millionaire', but in any society where the coinage functions in a system of exchange, or where coins are earned, this convention is unthinkable. Should we actually meet up with such a tribe and wish to trade with them, we would be foolish if we expected anything substantial in return for their coins. One might explain their behaviour in some other way, by drawing analogies with the business of tossing a horseshoe over one's shoulder, but then we would not be talking about coins in any sense of the word.

In this example the limits to spontaneity are not imposed by the natural facts but by the role which coinage plays in any society that has evolved beyond the apes. There is no point in this convention since its adoption into any currency system would be destructive of that system.[28]

Another of Wittgenstein's examples concerns a tribe who piled timber:

> in heaps of arbitrary, varying height and then sold it at a price proportionate to the area covered by the piles.

justifying this practice with the remark,

> Of course, if you buy more timber, you must pay more.
> (RFM.I.149).

Wittgenstein then imagines someone trying to convince them that they were wrong. He asks:

> How could I show them that - as I should say - you don't
> really buy more wood if you buy a pile covering a bigger
> area?..I should, for instance, take a pile which was small
> by their ideas and, by laying the logs around, change it
> into a 'big' one. This *might* convince them - but perhaps
> they would say: "Yes, now its a *lot* of wood and costs
> more" - and that would be the end of the matter....We should
> presumably say in this case: they simply do not mean the
> same by 'a lot of wood' and 'a little wood' as we do; and
> they have quite a different system of payment from us. (RFM.I.149)

Is it simply a matter of 'their having quite a different system of payment from us'? Is it correct to call it a system of payment in any sense? Or is it an activity that has been abstracted away from a wider social system? - a suggestion that Wittgenstein had not entirely freed himself from the atomist standpoint.

Questioning the intelligibility of Wittgenstein's example, Barry Stroud refers to the above mentioned example of the wood-sellers:

> Surely they would have us believe that a one-by-six-inch
> board all of a sudden increased in size or quantity when
> it was turned from resting on its one-inch edge to resting
> on its six-inch side. And what would the relation between
> quantity and weight possibly be for such people? A man
> could buy as much wood as he could possibly lift, only to
> find, upon dropping it, that he has just lifted more wood
> than he could possibly lift. Or is there more wood, but
> the same weight? Or perhaps these people do not understand
> the expression 'more' and 'less' at all. They must, if
> they can say, "Now it's a lot of wood and costs more". And
> do these people think of themselves as shrinking when they
> shift from standing on both feet to standing on one? Also,
> it would be possible for a house that is twice as large as
> another built on exactly the same plan to contain much less wood.
> How much wood is bought need have no connection with how
> much wood is needed for building the house. And so on.
> Problems involved in understanding what it would be like to
> sell wood in this way can be multiplied indefinitely.[29]

We should note also that Wittgenstein speaks of 'buying' and 'selling' the wood, as opposed to religious ritual. What sort of barter is it? Where, for instance, does the notion of an honest or dishonest deal come in? And would it not be possible for someone familiar with the 'normal' concept of measurement to swindle the members of this tribe? And if they were swindled it could only be attributed to their stupidity. Such conventions, when considered in the social daylight, are not really credible alternatives at all. But it is not the natural facts which makes these language games unacceptable. If a society wanted to accept such conventions there is nothing in the natural world that would prevent them. Yet if they were actually and consistently applied they would have to suffer the consequences. They would have to abandon all recognisable social, economic, practical and normal techniques.

A similar exercise in fanciful possibilities is to be found in an essay by Rush Rhees.[30] Adopting an example similar to that of Wittgenstein's elastic ruler (RFM.I.5), Rhees refers to the Eddie Cantor film, *Strike Me Pink*, where Eddie measures cloth with an elastic yardstick, using the extended yardstick when he is taking the cloth off the roll and when he is asking the customer: "Is that enough?" and using the shrunken yardstick when he cuts the cloth.[31] According to Rhees:

> It might be a universal practice to have elastic yardsticks, and further each person might pride himself on having his own special degree of elasticity in the yardstick he used. Business in such a community would be rather different to business in ours. But it might go on, and people might, if you asked them, give reasons for preferring it that way.[32]

But Rhees's main point is that:

> when we say that there is a justification or a reason for our measuring in the way we do, this does not mean that there could be no justification for measuring in any other way.[33]

What sort of justification could we offer for measuring in such a bizarre way? And why on earth would people 'prefer to do business this way'? What sort of business would it be? Presumably in that society one would have no need to concern oneself about the amount one obtained. The concept of an amount worth so much would be meaningless. A little would be as valuable as a lot. We would not be speaking of a society with any intelligible economy, so business could not 'go on' as Rhees maintains. This society would have to be such that concepts of linear measurement would be meaningless, unless they believed that the objects they wished to cover with their cloth continually changed their size.

Such people would not have the ability to manufacture the machines for making cloth, let alone cut and measure cloth. And they certainly would not have any idea how to cover things with cloth if by some miraculous way they found themselves in possession of cloth.

Now the limitations on the arbitrariness of this convention are not the natural facts, as one might at first suspect. It is vaguely possible for some humanoid species to exist and have what might approximate to this concept of measurement. But they would not be in any respect similar to the people we would expect to meet anywhere on this Earth. They would live nakedly in a world without man-made products, having no tools or weapons based on any concept of precision. What would count as the limitations of the arbitrariness of such a convention is the fact that if we adopt such a fundamental change in our concept of linear measurement we would be forced into a progressive abandonment of almost every other convention in society. It is in this way that conventions form a system acting as an essential support for each other. To grasp how language and reality are mediated in human conventions one must arrive at an understanding of the ways in which the various conventions rest on each other and not on some external foundation. Unless one were to envisage a total collapse of an entire system of human institutions the adoption of Eddie Cantor's system of measurement is untenable. And precisely because it counts as an example of the outrageously unthinkable, precisely because it is a system which cannot be integrated with other systems, it has a place within the comic productions of the Hollywood film genre. Eddie Cantor's mathematics, like his dance routines, is a product of the American dream machine and for that reason has no place in the real world. It was never intended to supplement or replace our normal methods of 'going on with one's business'.

The antidote for unlimited conventionalism is to consider human beings as actors, not as spectators. This was fundamental to Hegel's account of truth and recognised on many occasions by Wittgenstein, and one can only conclude that his own over-emphasis of the moment of conventionalism expresses little more than a desire to break the hold of a realist ontology. For once we imagine human beings actually applying some of the conventions he suggests they seldom appear as credible alternatives. The same point can be applied to Plato's famous cave allegory. If the prisoners in the cave were capable of acting instead of watching, they would soon find the limits to the arbitrariness in the drawing up of conventions concerning the shadows on the wall. If they are to participate in the performance their conventions must give some support to each other.

One of the peculiar features of a highly complex society is the way in which the various conventions prop each other up. The extent of these interconnections often reveal how many limitations there are to the drawing up of a new language game. These limitations have little to do with any allegedly natural base or foundation but are imposed by the relationships between the conventions within an overall system. This point can be illustrated by the following example of an attempt to change what would seem to be an apparently minor convention. Referring to the phenomenon of 'Dynamic Conservatism' Donald Schon says:

> An issue of considerable liveliness in the Department of Commerce, for example, was whether standards for bathtubs cover resistance to cigarette burns. The issue appeared trivial until it became apparent that this specification ruled out fibreglass-reinforced polyester, the major competitor to the traditional porcelain enamel bathtub. A lobby for the cigarette-burn-resistance-requirement had emerged which included, not surprisingly, the makers of porcelain enamel tubs, the related unions, the steel-makers and their associations. The conflict engaged vested interests in the old and the new technologies; and the representatives of the old were at the time stronger, more entrenched, and more effective in working their will through government.[34]

An even more striking example concerns the attempt to initiate a minor change in the conventions governing timber standards which, incidentally, reflects on the absurdity of Wittgenstein's wood-sellers. According to Schon:

> The literal '2 by 4' had long been out of date. The question now was whether boards marked '2 by 4' should have a thickness of $1\frac{1}{2}$ inches measured at the fixed moisture content, or whether the thickness should be $1\frac{5}{8}$ without specification of moisture content.

> This seemed one of the less passionate issues of the day, but it ended up generating approximately 30,000 letters per year - more than any other issue in the recent history of the Department of Commerce. It divided the country into 'wets' and 'drys'. The drys were those few lumber manufacturers large enough to afford a kiln, so that they could make kiln-dried lumber to dimension. And the wets were those tens of thousands of lumber manufacturers too small to afford kiln drying equipment; because they could not afford it, they would not have been able to meet the new standard.

> The standard would, in all likelihood, have eliminated thousands of small producers. It would have shifted the regional balance of lumber production; and it would, it was

rumoured, have added approximately 5,000 million dollars to the value of Weyerhauser's timber holdings, simply by enabling that firm to make a greater number of 2 by 4's from a single tree.

The battle over lumber standards drew in all components of the building industry, a full range of Federal agencies, State governments from Maine to North Carolina, and Congressional representatives to boot; Magnusson and Jackson from Washington, not surprisingly, represented the large 'dry' manufacturers; James Roosevelt, at the time a representative from Southern California, took up the cause of the many small lumber manufacturers in that region. Speeches were delivered on the floor of the House. Many closed door sessions were held. Accusations of illegitimate influence were bandied about. And the entire issue took up more of the time of the officials in the Department of Commerce than I have the means of computing. The intensity of the struggle grew out of the fact that the dynamic conservatism of the industry was threatened, not by a fragile outside force, but by a considerable internal one.35

When one is prepared to consider what is involved in adopting a different set of conventions it is clear that there are very definite limits to the arbitrariness in drawing up a new language game. Not anything, for example, will count as a belief. In his later works Wittgenstein is very clear on this issue: like Hegel, Wittgenstein later accepted that beliefs have to belong to a system.

Might I not believe that once, without knowing it, perhaps in a state of unconsciousness, I was taken far away from the earth - that other people even know this, but do not mention it to me? But this would not fit in with the rest of my convictions at all. Not that I could describe the system of these convictions. Yet my convictions do form a system, a structure. (OC.102)

The limitations to the spontaneity in the drawing up of a new language game are not the facts themselves but the system in which the facts are organised together with other conventions, moral and political norms, and so on. In the above passage Wittgenstein is calling attention to the interaction of beliefs rather than their grounds; their organisation rather than their foundations. Although Wittgenstein did not explicitly say so, morality and politics play an important organising role in the drawing up of new language games. For example, consider the difficulties entailed in the attempt to 'return to nature', or to reconstruct the existence of a fourteenth-century peasant. Even if one were able to create identical material conditions there would remain one vital difference, namely the moral problems involved in the decision to turn

one's back on the advantages of 20th century life, for example, peni-
cillin. Such problems would not be found in the consciousness of a
fourteenth-century peasant.

7. AGREEMENT IN 'FORM OF LIFE'

The truth is only realised in the form of a system. [Hegel,
PG.MM.28/B.85]

In our examination of those examples where Wittgenstein over-empha-
sised the moment of conventionality the technique was essentially
Hegelian. By themselves the alternative language games were one-sided
and abstract. Having outlined the concrete actuality, by taking them
seriously, we have shown how such alternative systems are self-defea-
ting. What has been negated is the 'abstract' distinction between
nature and convention; that if language is not anchored to the natural
facts it must be conventional. But against this assumption it has
been argued that the limitations to conventionality are to be found in
the relationships with other conventions which form an interrelated
system, or network of concepts. For these reasons not anything will
count as a language game. Only if we have a specific point can we
effect a decisive change in the conventions and social norms which
underlie grammatical rules. Having a point is bound up with what one
can, at a given time in history and economic and technical development,
count as a point.

We are now in a position to indicate the nature of the answer to the
question 'From where does language derive its necessity if it is not
read off from the natural facts?' The alternative to foundationalism
appeared to lie in a programme of 'full-blooded conventionalism'. But,
as we have indicated, there does exist another alternative. Conventions are limited by their role within a system, by human beings and
their history, institutions, and social practices.[36] If we want to
understand the nature of things we must understand language, but to
understand language we must not look for foundations but at the system
in which words and things are assigned a role. In making the necessity
of language dependent upon 'forms of life' Wittgenstein was approaching
this position:

'So you are saying that human agreement decides what is true
and what is false?' - It is what human beings *say* that is true
and false; and they agree in the *language* they use. That is
not agreement in opinions but in form of life. (PI.241)

But Wittgenstein never specified any form of life; nowhere does he
make any contribution to an understanding of the political and social
bases which are central to an understanding of the relationship between

human beings and the world, although in many ways he did recognise that ethical principles had an equally important contribution to our understanding of reality as epistemological principles. In a very important sense Hegel goes beyond Wittgenstein. Hegel for his part rejected what the atomists have said about the foundations of language by showing how participation in the concrete universal (objective or intersubjective spirit) is epistemologically prior to the alleged immediate certainty of sensory particulars. 'This bare fact of certainty, however, is really and admittedly the abstractest and poorest kind of truth'. (PG. MM.82/B.149) Like Wittgenstein, Hegel draws attention to the fact that sense experience itself is dependent upon a wealth of institutionalised practices, culture and training, and to deny this is to engage in a most 'abstract' enterprise which illicitly ignores the system of relations in which a reference to sense immediacy is made. Thus having rejected the 'contemplative' approach to epistemology Hegel attempted to provide the concrete content to the circumstances in which human beings actually operate upon reality. When Hegel says that 'Before real activity nothing truly exists' (GPII.MM.215/H.197) he is prepared to say something about the nature of this activity. For this reason the Hegelian enterprise must undertake to show how the various practices and social conventions in human life, together with their philosophical expressions, form an organic and systematic totality.

NOTES

[1] J. Hartnack, *Wittgenstein and Modern Philosophy* trans. M. Cranston, New York: Anchor Books, Doubleday & Co. 1965, p.ix.

[2] B. Russell, *An Inquiry into Meaning and Truth,* London: Allen & Unwin, 1940, p.64.

[3] Since the volume of works on Wittgenstein's 'Private Language Argument' are numerous to the point of becoming a separate discipline itself, I have not attempted any detailed analysis here. The two most influential papers on this subject are 'Can there be a Private Language?' by A. J. Ayer, and another sharing the same title by Rush Rhees in *Wittgenstein,* edited by G. Pitcher, London: Macmillan, 1968.

[4] G. G. Simpson, *Principles of Animal Taxonomy,* New York: Columbia University, 1961. p.2.

[5] Ibid, p.3.

[6] B. Russell, *History of Western Philosophy,* London: Allen &
Unwin, 1946. p.712.

[7] Ibid. pp.714-5.

[8] P. Winch, *The Idea of a Social Science,* London: Routledge, 1959.
pp.27-9.

[9] E. K. Specht, *The Foundations of Wittgenstein's Late Philosophy,*
trans. D. E. Watford, Manchester: University Press, 1969. p.140.
The same point is made by Sartre when he says that 'Language is
praxis as practical relation of one man to another and *praxis* is
always language (whether it lies or whether it tells the truth)
because it cannot be spoken without meaning. Languages are the
products of history; as such each one finds exteriority and unity
of separation'. *Critique de la Raison Dialectique,* Book 1,
Section B, from an unpublished translation by A. R. Manser,
University of Southampton.

[10] Specht. op. cit. p.142.

[11] Ibid. p.142.

[12] The interest in a 'grammar of material', for example, why we speak
of 'artificial limbs' but 'false teeth', typified in Hegel's eyes,
the kind of empiricism that passes for philosophy in England. (See
Enz.1.7) For Hegel philosophy is more than the recording of facts,
such as the discovery of 'some sixty species of parrots, one hundred and thirty seven species of veronica and so forth'. (L.II.MM.
375/J&S.320) Philosophy involves a principle for the comprehension of the facts and an understanding of what this principle
means to those who hold it. Thus for Hegel - and this is true for
Wittgenstein - language, like any other object of interest to the
philosopher, can only be studied philosophically if one is prepared to go beyond the material content.

[13] See PI.354, 373 and 496.

[14] In fact the US Indians fought a long and protracted battle to be
recognised as 'persons' in the legal sense. See, for example, the
civil action of *Standing Bear v. Crook,* April 1879, a landmark in
American legal history, where Standing Bear won, for a limited
period, the right to be considered a 'person'.

[15] Specht. op cit. p.159.

[16] C. I. Lewis 'A Pragmatic Conception of the *A Priori*' in the
Journal of Philosophy, 20. 1923.

[17] It should be noted that Wittgenstein is not so much advancing a
theory of language as removing a misleading picture.

[18] 'Wittgenstein's Philosophy of Mathematics' in *Wittgenstein,* ed.
Pitcher. op cit. pp.425-6.

[19] G. E. Moore, *Philosophical Papers,* London: Allen & Unwin, 1959. p.259.

[20] F. Ferre, 'Colour Incompatability and Language Games', *Mind,* 1961.

[21] Ibid p.94.

[22] Ibid p.94.

[23] Specht. op cit. p.170.

[24] It is important to note that Wittgenstein was not simply substi-tuting rules for facts as the foundations of language. In his *Lecture Notes* Moore points out that this attitude would still re-flect the desire for a subject for every substantive. Says Moore, "although he had said, at least once, that the meaning of a word was 'constituted' by the grammatical rules which applied to it, he explained later that he did not mean that the meaning of a word *was* a list of rules; and he said that though a word 'carried' its meaning with it, it did not carry with it the grammatical rules which applied to it. He said that the student who asked him whether he meant that the meaning of a word *was* a list of rules would not have been tempted to ask the question but for the false idea (which he held to be a common one) that in the case of a substantive like 'the meaning' you have to look at something at which you can point and say 'This is the meaning'". *Philosophical Papers,* p.258.

[25] I believe that stressing the point, rather than the facts, as the limits to spontaneity, finds support in many of Wittgenstein's remarks on necessity. For example, PI.120, 142, 545, 564, 567.

[26] Specht.op cit. p.172.

[27] Ibid p.172.

[28] Should hyper-inflation cause trading stamps to have a greater value than sterling, it is quite conceivable that we could have the convention of which Wittgenstein speaks concerning the now worthless coinage. But in that case we would not leave trading stamps (the reliable coinage) on the ground for others to pick up.

[29] Barry Stroud, 'Wittgenstein and Logical Necessity', *Wittgenstein,* ed. Pitcher, pp.487-8.

[30] Rush Rhees, *Discussion of Wittgenstein,* London: Routledge. 1970.

[31] Ibid pp.121-2.

[32] Ibid p.122.

[33] Ibid p.122.

[34] Donald Schon, *Beyond the Stable State,* Middlesex: Penguin, 1973.
      p.226.

[35] Ibid pp.226-7.

[36] Wittgenstein's conception of system is similar to Hegel's, but
      this analogy was far from the minds of Wittgenstein's contempora-
      ries, which is why his assertion that 'Every symbol must belong
      to a system', (quoted by Moore, *Philosophical Papers,* p.259) was
      unclear to Moore. Says Moore: "The word 'system' was one which
      he used frequently, and I don't know what condition he would have
      held must be satisfied by different signs in order that they may
      be properly be said to belong to the same 'system'". (Ibid p.259)

II Gestures and social life

1. HEGEL AND WITTGENSTEIN ON POINTING AND UNDERSTANDING

One can refer to an object when speaking by pointing to it.
Here pointing is part of the language game.
[Wittgenstein, PI.669]

Discussing sense-certainty in the *Phenomenology,* Hegel portrays the sensory realist adopting a subjective and solipsistic standpoint. Like Wittgenstein, Hegel sees solipsism and subjective idealism as doctrines sharing the assumptions of passive empiricism. Failing to find certainty in the object, the consciousness depicted by Hegel seeks certainty in subjective experience, saying that 'No matter what is said about the universal significance of symbols at least *I* know what I mean when I point to a given object'. But, as Hegel demonstrates, outside of a shared system of rules and conventions there can be no meaningful expression of this certainty. The retreat into solipsism by Hegel's sensory realist, and Hegel's treatment of this position, reveals more than a family resemblance to Wittgenstein's account of human language. Hegel's solipsist has no use for language, privately enjoying sensuous objects, like a pre-linguistic Robinson Crusoe. Solipsism, when taken seriously, abandons discourse. Hegel presents a consciousness standing outside of language in a state of pure solipsism, having intuitions and feelings, but nothing more, and asks us to consider how this consciousness might indicate a datum of sense immediacy with a pointing gesture.

This enables Hegel to pin·down one of the deepest-held assumptions of realism, that the act of pointing has priority over language. ·A consciousness is therefore presented holding the view that language, being universal, can somehow distort one's meaning, that language stands as a barrier between the subject and object of experience. On these terms it would appear that a more immediate and unambiguous reference can be made in the absence of language. Hegel invites the reader of the *Phenomenology* to step into the shoes of the sensory realist and attempt to indicate the bare particular 'here' of sense immediacy with a pointing gesture. However, as Hegel demonstrates, it soon becomes apparent that 'the very act of pointing out proves not to be immediate knowledge' but is mediated through a whole process of universal concepts. (PG.MM. 90/B.157) In fact the mere act of pointing presupposes a familiarity with a wide range of sophisticated spatio-temporal concepts. Thus:

The here pointed out, which I keep hold of, is likewise a *this* here which, in fact, is not *this here*, but a before and a behind, an above and below, a right and a left. The above is itself likewise this manifold otherness - above, below, etc. The here, which was to be pointed out, disappears in other heres, and these disappear similarly. What is pointed out, holds fast, and is permanent, is a negative this, which only is so when the heres are taken as they should be. (PG.MM.89-90 /B.157)

The force of Hegel's argument can be appreciated in the light of Wittgenstein's account of the role of pointing and gestures within a 'form of life' to which we shall now turn. Like Hegel, Wittgenstein (PI.1-42) shows how the act of giving an ostensive definition does not have any foundational role in the acquisition of language but presupposes a familiarity with a linguistic system. We do not begin with pointing and gestures since it is necessary to know what one is pointing at together with the significance of pointing. Pointing and gestures are themselves part of language. A child has to be taught the significance of pointing just as he has to be taught the significance of words.

The act of pointing is usually that of holding an arm outstretched with one finger, usually the forefinger, extended. But why should this act alone be taken as the indication of an object? One could, as Wittgenstein argues, be indicating its surface or colour. Consider some other actions that one might be performing with these physical movements:

    a. Giving directions to a motorist - not pointing to something on the front of his car.

    b. Signalling the commencement of an execution by firing squad.

    c. Giving a batsman 'out' in a game of cricket.

    d. Sending a footballer off the field - or maybe the whole team - or signalling half-time.

    e. Showing the doctor an injured finger.

    f. Illustrating an example of ostensive definition in a philosophy lecture.

    g. Identifying the accused in an identity parade.

    h. Making a protest.

Out of the above eight examples only 5 and 7 count as pointing in the sense that something in the visual field is being indicated. The other examples are clearly bound up with a system of conventions and human practices. It is not so clear, for many philosophers, whether indicative pointing falls into the same category. In the above examples it should be clear that the act of pointing alone is meaningless; it is the context which determines the sense in which one can be said to be pointing, or to be able to recognise what one is pointing at. Unless we share a number of conventions and have many interests in common, the mere stretching of an arm is meaningless. Consider Wittgenstein's example of the arrow:

> How does it come about that this arrow → points? Doesn't it seem to carry something besides itself? - 'No, not the dead line on paper; only the psychical thing, the meaning can do that'. - That is both true and false. The arrow points only in the application that a living being makes of it. (PI.454)

Moreover, not all indicative pointing is done with the arm and fingers. A flicker of the eyes, the slightest turning of the head, can often be a form of indicating the required area of attention. As long as the convention is shared we can indicate objects in various ways. It is possible to imagine a society where indicative pointing, as we know it, carries with it some form of taboo - just as it is considered a form of rudeness to point at someone in public, or point one's finger in the face of the person one is addressing.

However, indicative pointing does recur in different cultures, even though the actual spoken languages differ considerably. This means nothing more than the fact that the rules for the use of certain gestures are less conventional and spontaneous than those of spoken languages. It is possible for a child to be trained to indicate objects by means of some peculiar movement of the left knee, and it is possible for a whole society to have different conventions regarding indicative pointing. But generally when two strangers meet and discover themselves to lack a common language, they can indicate objects by pointing as we do.

For various reasons philosophers have been tempted to make too rigid a distinction between the spoken language and gestures, seeing the latter as something more basic than the former. The picture here is of a traveller communicating with the natives by means of gestures until he eventually connects the objects indicated with the sounds accompanying the gestures. But in making this distinction one ignores the fact that the gestures are themselves rule-governed activities, and determined according to the context within which they are made. A greater variation amongst cultures in linguistic conventions than in gestures does not prove that gestures are, in some sense, more basic and real; it merely shows that certain societies may share similar gestures whilst having different spoken languages. The traveller who makes what he thinks to be a universal gesture of peace and love to a primitive tribe might very well pay dearly for his error if his gesture corresponds to something which is considered an insult by members of that tribe.

When the traveller attempts to communicate with signs and gestures it is not the case that he is using a more basic form of communication, foolproof and independent of language and culture; he is anticipating the types of gesture that would be familiar to the tribe he hopes to communicate with. And this presupposes a certain familiarity with primitive tribes in general and an ability to understand that certain concepts, important in his own society, might be meaningless in this one. His choice of gestures would reveal that he was not starting from absolute beginnings, without any preconceived notion of communication, without a spoken language. It would be of little use, for instance, if an explorer confronted a primitive tribe with gestures indicating his need for a television set. Such a set of gestures would be clearly unfamiliar to the tribe. He may begin by touching his mouth to indicate food, but then he might have to make further distinctions between liquids and solids and so forth. Initial steps of communication would be rough and ready, depending on the traveller's knowledge of the tribe he wishes to communicate with. If he knew they were a hunting community he might fashion his gestures according to his concept of the gestures appropriate to such a community.

That it is possible to communicate with another tribe, whose spoken language differs from ours, is not because of any basic activity such as gestures, which could vary according to the interests of that society. The only criterion for the determination of the validity of one's interpretation of an alien language is the consistency with which sounds and gestures are applied. To grasp the consistent application of the rules employed presupposes that one already possesses considerable knowledge of the life-style one is attempting to interpret, since it assumes that one can, at least, recognise the objects and activities that one is attempting to associate with the spoken words or gestures. Consider, for example, learning their equivalent of the word 'cure'. I can only tell if it is being consistently applied if I can recognise what counts as a cure in the society I am investigating. But my recognition would only be possible if I were able to recognise other activities associated with cures, such as symptoms of illness, worry, anxiety, and gratitude shown towards the healer. A concept can only be understood against a common way of life. For this reason if a stone could make sounds we could not understand it - for no other reason than the fact that we could not understand the way of life of a stone. Wittgenstein makes a similar point when he says 'if a lion could talk we could not understand him'. (PI.454) When we attempt to understand an alien society it might be true that we cannot, in the first instance,

32

understand their words and gestures. But when we begin to interpret them we must have already obtained a considerable knowledge of that society.

There is, however, a strand in Wittgenstein's thought where he correctly denies that gestures have a necessary similarity, but he over-emphasises the moment of conventionality when he imagines the possibility of a tribe that cannot be understood. For example:

> ...one human being can be a complete enigma to another. We learn this when we come into a strange country with entirely strange traditions; and what is more, even given a mastery of the country's language. We do not *understand* the people. (And not because of not knowing what they are saying to themselves). We cannot find our feet with them. (PI.II.xi)

Where would one go to find such a tribe? Wittgenstein is misleading in the above passage since it is unlikely that one could master a country's language without understanding quite a lot about the life-style of its inhabitants. Moreover, if one human was a complete enigma to another they would not acknowledge each other as humans. This is what Sartre has in mind in the following passage:

> It is necessary that the master has confidence in man in the person of his slaves; the contradiction of racism and colonialism and all forms of tyranny is known; to treat a man like a dog he must first be recognized as a man. The secret sickness of the master is that he is perpetually compelled to take into consideration the *human reality* in his slaves (whether he relies on their skill or on their synthetic comprehension of work situations, or whether he takes precautions against permanent possibility of revolt or an escape) at the same time as refusing the political and economic status which *at that time* defines human beings.[1]

Sartre's point is that the master actually sees his slaves as men not as things even though he treats them as things. To treat them as things, or sub-human,is to recognise them as men. Oppression, he says, 'consists in...treating the other as an animal',[2] as opposed to believing the other to be an animal. To treat a person as an animal or a thing is to deny what is entitled to them as men, but this is still to see them as human. 'Animality', says Sartre, 'Is imposed on the slave by the master *after* the recognition of his humanity'.[3] For example:

> It is known that the American plantation owners in the 17th century refused to allow black children to be educated in the Christian religion in order to preserve the right to treat

them as sub-men. That was implicitly to recognise that they were *already* men: the proof is that they only differed from their masters by a religious faith which it was admitted they were capable of acquiring by the very care that was taken to forbid it to them.[4]

If you do not take the other to be human, if he is a 'complete enigma', then you do not feel it necessary to take steps to deny him the possibility of demonstrating his equal right to the claim to possess manhood One can only discriminate against those we recognise as humans. For this reason there are no regulations against the admission of artifacts or stones to the universities, whilst there are universities in the world who deny admission to allegedly 'inferior' races. To take these measures acknowledges their essential humanity.

Now Wittgenstein's example of one human being being a complete enigma to another has a definite air of unreality about it. This strange society is more akin to those depicted in the wild and dubious tales of sixteenth-century sailors than in the investigations of contemporary anthropology. For when a modern explorer confronts an alien society, he is already prepared to meet a different set of traditions. He has probably travelled many miles, studied the area, learnt something about primitive tribes in general, and may even hold a degree in anthropology or primitive languages. He has an idea of what to look for. It would be different if he had tumbled out of bed one Kafkaesque morning to dis cover himself in an alien society. Confronting an alien society is not that kind of sudden culture shock - although there may still be a shock For this reason the explorer can observe their mannerisms and eventuall come to an understanding of them. He may make mistakes, but if they are human, and have a language, he cannot find them such an enigma: it must be possible for him to understand - though not necessarily approve - a great deal about them. To understand a language one needs to under stand how that language is used and how to correlate the application of its words to the actions within that form of life. For this reason if two forms of life are entirely dissimilar - that is, a non-human con fronting a human one - we could not begin such an enquiry. And this is what Wittgenstein must have had in mind when he said elsewhere:

If you went to Mars and men were spheres with sticks coming out, you wouldn't know what to look for. (LC.2)

So far it has been maintained that knowing a language entails having some knowledge about its users. If we can communicate with an alien society it is not because there is a common stock of human gestures which serve as a foundation of language, but because there are certain basic similarities between different life-styles. That is to say, the difference between the most diverse human societies is never so great

as the difference between any human society and a hive of bees. For
this reason Wittgenstein is correct - as opposed to his suggestion that
one human being can be an enigma to another - when he says:

> Suppose you come as an explorer into a strange country with
> a language quite strange to you. In what circumstances would
> you say the people there gave orders, understood them, obeyed
> them, rebelled against them, and so on? The common behaviour
> of mankind is the system of references by which we interpret
> an unknown language. (PI.206)

To understand a language involves some knowledge of the 'common behaviour
of mankind'. It has been argued that this involves knowing something
about the way of life of its users. Can we know a language, as Wittgenstein implies in the *Investigations* (II.xi), without knowing anything
about its users? Is this consistent with the main thrust of Wittgenstein's thought in his later writings?

2.   IS A FORM OF LIFE A WAY OF LIFE?

> ...anyone who did not know the history of the city, the culture,
> and the laws of Athens could almost have learned them from the
> festivals if they had lived a year within its gates. [Hegel,
> *Early Theological Writings,* p.147]

Another way of posing the above question is to ask whether I can imagine
a language without imagining a 'way of life'? In the following quo-
tations it is evident that Wittgenstein actually held that the possibility of imagining a language is indistinguishable from the possibility
of imagining a form of life.

a. It is easy to imagine a language consisting only of orders and
    reports in battle...And to imagine a language means to imagine
    a form of life. (PI.19)

b. Here the term 'language *game*' is meant to bring into prominence
    the fact that *speaking* of language is part of an activity, or of a
    form of life. (PI.23)

c. 'So you are saying that human agreement decides what is true
    and what is false'? - It is what human beings *say* that is
    true and false; and they agree in the language they use. That
    is not agreement in opinions but in form of life. (PI.241)

d. Can only those hope who can talk? Only those who have mastered
    the use of a language. That is to say the phenomena of hope
    are modes of this complicated form of life. (PI.II.1)

e. It is no doubt true that if you could not calculate with
    certain sorts of paper and ink, if, that is, they were
    subject to certain queer changes - but still the fact that
    they changed could in turn only be got from memory and
    comparison with other means of calculation. And how are
    these tested in their turn? What has to be accepted, the
    given, is - so one could say - *forms of life*. (PI.II.xi)

f. Now I would like to regard this certainty, not as something
    akin to hastiness or superficiality, but as a form of life.
    (OC.358)

Exactly what Wittgenstein meant by the expression 'form of life' is
far from clear. Is a way of life, for example, the same as a form of
life? Is the possibility of imagining a different way of life bound up
with the possibility of imagining a different language? Can we imagine
a different language without imagining a different way of life in the
sense that Wittgenstein employs the expression 'form of life' in the
Investigations 19?

In a paper concerned with Wittgenstein's concept of a 'form of life'
J. F. M. Hunter[5] implicitly distinguishes between a way of life and a
form of life when he agrees with Wittgenstein that we cannot imagine
another language without imagining another form of life but he argues
that we can imagine a different language without having to imagine a
different way of life. His conclusion is that a form of life in Wittgenstein's sense, is not equivalent to a way of life. As our concern
is only with Hunter's arguments for the distinction between a form of
life and a way of life his own conception of a form of life will not be
considered here.

Hunter sets up four interpretations of Wittgenstein's 'form of life'
three of which he rejects. The relevant one for our discussion is the
third interpretation which, according to Hunter, mistakenly equates a
form of life with a 'way of life or a mode, manner, fashion, or style
of life: that has something to do with the class structure, the values
the religion, the types of industry and commerce and of recreation that
characterise a group of people'.[6] In what follows these remarks will
be accepted as a working definition of a way of life.

Hunter's reasons for 'not treating a way of life as a serious conten-
der'[7] for a form of life in the sense expressed in the *Investigations*
19 are two-fold. The first example he offers is that of Wittgenstein's
builders: 'What do we know of the way of life of the builders discussed in *Investigations* 2?', asks Hunter.[8] Presumably Hunter is claiming
that it is possible to imagine that the builders do have a language,
one which exists independently of their way of life but not of their

form of life. Whether or not the builders have a language, and whether Wittgenstein intended these remarks as a description of a language game has been discussed by Rush Rhees in his paper on 'Wittgenstein's Builders'.[9]

In this paper Rhees argues that Wittgenstein's analogies between games and language serve as explanations of the working of the latter, but that the explanation is a philosophical one. This presents difficulties of the sort that Hunter does not see. According to Rhees, Wittgenstein "gives an analogy when he refers to the explanation of a 'game', but it is never more than an analogy, and at times we may feel unsure just how to take it".[10] So when Wittgenstein speaks of the builders' language game, the analogy he is providing is a very peculiar one. It is one of the many examples designed to show what a language is. These language games, argues Rhees, are not intended to serve as examples of complete languages. But this seems to be contradicted by Wittgenstein, who says, in the *Brown Book*, that the various language games are not incomplete parts of language, 'but as languages complete in themselves, as complete systems of human communication'. (BB.81) On the surface this would appear to fortify Hunter's contentions.

It should be remarked, however, that many of Wittgenstein's remarks carry what can be described as a negative force. In other words, whilst not being positive accounts of language and reality, they negate certain misleading assumptions concerning the nature of language. For this reason the above remark from the *Brown Book* should be taken negatively as a prophylactic against the *Tractatus* view that it should be possible to calculate all the possible forms of a proposition.

Now it is difficult to see what light the builders analogy sheds on the nature of language. Suppose we try to imagine a group of builders having only the expressions 'slab', 'beam', and so on. What sort of building site is this? It is an interesting, but scarcely observed, fact that on a real building site in the United Kingdom the expressions 'Bricks', 'Mortar', 'Sand', and so on, uttered in isolation signify periods of tension. Such expressions are uttered to let it be known that someone, such as a labourer, has failed to maintain an adequate supply of materials. They signify a convention for revealing that he is not 'up to his job', which can be seen by the labourer in question as a direct insult, or worse, an informal means of informing the management of his inadequacy. It is clear that far from being elementary expressions in actual usage 'Bricks', 'Mortar' etc., are permeated with economic and political concepts. Given the power relationships within industry their utterance can lead to a dismissal or conversely a stoppage. Their usage is far from that of a simple language game: it invokes the entire spectrum of a class-divided society and the nature of industrial relations.

Let us abstract the superstructure away and imagine a site where this
was the only employment of language. What happens when they encounter
snags, what would count as a misunderstanding, how would they correct
someone who passed a beam every time they called 'Slab'? How would
they know when someone had grasped the rule for the application of the
limited number of expressions in their vocabulary? Rhees, quite rightly, has doubts whether a genuine language is being spoken in this example. 'The trouble', he says, 'is not to imagine a people with a
limited vocabulary. The trouble is to imagine that they spoke the
language only to give these special orders on the job and otherwise
never spoke at all. I do not think it would be speaking a language'.[1]

On Hunter's account they do speak a language, however restricted, and
that knowledge of this language is independent of any knowledge of their
way of life. Yet if we reflect on the actual working of this language
it would soon become evident that no one could ever speak it. Another
way of describing this language would be to say that it was a language
without conversation. To be sure they utter orders and react to them,
but how do they exchange information in this language? If we met one
of these builders how could we ask him anything? How could he tell us
anything? When we learn to speak we learn how to tell people something
however inarticulate our efforts may appear. We learn what it makes
sense to say, what certain remarks mean to certain people, and how our
remarks have a bearing on one another. Learning to speak is learning
to argue, to convince, to follow a conversation, and mislead or be mis-
led.

Hunter's second example consists of referring to an imaginary language in which there are no orders; a variant on Wittgenstein's theme
in paragraph 19 of the *Investigations*. Hunter claims that whilst the
society employing this language would differ from ours, the possibility of imagining such a language is independent of any knowledge of
their way of life. Says Hunter:

> More generally, if I imagine a language with, for example,
> no orders, all I know for certain is that the manner of life
> of the users of that language would be quite different from
> ours. I do not know whether they would find ways of training
> people to do what needs to be done without being told, or
> whether they would resign themselves to not getting done what
> we would normally achieve by such methods as giving orders.
> Even if I could reach some conclusions about this, it is
> still true that I first imagined the language independently
> of the manner of life, and then drew my conclusions as to
> what manner of life is entailed.[12]

What is it that makes Hunter so certain that he is able to imagine a language containing no orders at all? Or, for that matter what sort of language is Wittgenstein alleged to have in mind when he imagines one consisting entirely of orders? Nowhere does Hunter specify what would meet the satisfactory conditions of a language, nor could he, since languages are not the kind of things that can be categorised and classified apart from human activity.

Presumably Hunter will agree that not anything will count as a language; that is to say, not anything we can imagine will count as a language. The sound of a dripping tap, a creaking door, or of a stick being dragged along some iron railings would not, in any sense, be candidates for an imaginary language. We might rely on these sounds to symbolise something, say in a movie, where a close-up of a dripping tap together with appropriate sound effects, can be used to symbolise the state of mind of one of the characters. Such symbolism is not a language itself, but a mere part of language. For a set of sounds to serve as a meaningful symbol they have to have some meaning within the way of life of those to whom the symbolic expression is directed.

If we cannot imagine anything and call it a language what are the limits to the imagination in this field? Clearly the limits must be determined by the possibility, or impossibility, of a community adopting an imagined language. In this respect it is quite conceivable to imagine - or even discover - a language having no use for the word 'sepia'. On the other hand could we imagine a language which has no way of distinguishing truth from falsehood, correct from incorrect? Obviously not, since a language which has no concept of a mistake would have no criterion by which it could judge whether its own rules were being applied correctly. No one would ever know if he had learnt to speak it. Consistency, and with it, all communication would be non-existent. So if someone should claim to have imagined such a language, we would be justified in telling him that if it were seriously adopted, communication within it, and the possibility of translating it, would be ruled out, and for that reason whatever he had imagined could not be described as a language. Why not? Because there is no conceivable way in which it could be applied, or learnt. And if no community could adopt it then we could not say that it was a language in any sense of the word.

Hunter admits that a radically different language would entail a different way of life. What I suspect he is not aware of are the limitations to the possibility of drawing up a radically different language. He says of his imagined language in which no orders are given: 'We would have to have a society with a very different industrial, commercial, military, and family structure'.[13] But could any society exist which used the kind of language he claims to have imagined? If it cannot be adopted by any existing, or imagined society, then is it really a different language?

Can we adopt a language in which no orders are given, even with sufficient willingness on behalf of the people concerned? Alternatively, can we with a sufficient will, adopt or imagine anyone adopting a language consisting entirely of orders?

Consider the first possibility. Certainly Hunter is correct when he points out that given a linguistic change we cannot predict, with absolute exactness, the accompanying social change. But if one is imagining a change of such magnitude as this, we could predict that many institutions, as well as the army, industry and the family, would disappear. It would entail a radical departure from the way that everything is conducted in our lives: from the midwife's orders to the undertaker's. It would involve drastic changes in the way that children are educated and trained: not in the sense of a change from grammar schools to comprehensive schools, but from learning by being told to do it to somehow acquiring knowledge without instructions, without being trained in the use of language, without being trained in the most basic activities such as learning to walk. One would have to acquire the distinction between right and wrong, correct and incorrect without ever being told not to do anything or to do certain things the correct way.

Towards the end of the famous dialectic of the Master and Slave in the *Phenomenology*, Hegel makes some penetrating remarks concerning the importance of training and its relationship to the potential hegemony of the slave's consciousness. According to Hegel, if the slave is to triumph, forming himself through work, he must experience fear. 'The fear of the Lord is the beginning of wisdom', says Hegel, punning on the term 'lord', (PG.MM.153/B.238) and this wisdom is only attained when one is said to possess 'a mind of his own'.(PG.MM.154/B.239) Essential to this process are the moments of Fear and Service whose fusion is necessary for (a) the formative activity of shaping the objects of the natural world, acquiring skills and so on, and (b) developing confidence in oneself, learning that the processes of production do not depend upon another's powers and so on. Why is it that these two moments of Fear and Service are equally necessary?

Consider, for example, fear without service. Hegel depicts this in consciousness that remains 'formal', 'inward and mute'. (PG.MM.154/B.239) Fear without purpose will only produce a mindless slave, and by analogy the child who is merely frightened will never display a character of its own. On the other hand service without any fear - the libertarian standpoint pushed to its extreme - invariably produces the kind of consciousness that is said to have a 'vain and futile mind of its own'. (PG.MM.154/B.240) Hegel's point is that he who has never

experienced fear and discipline, just 'some slight anxiety' (ibid.),
cannot be said to 'have a mind of his own': he experiences a type of
freedom that does not get 'beyond the attitude of bondage'. (Ibid)[14]
He who has not acquired the discipline of social life is a slave to his
passions. A society without any form of training, without any means of
telling someone to do so and so, would breed some very queer and unfamiliar emotions. Such human emotions as mistrust, fear of punishment
however slight, and respect for authority legitimate or illegitimate,
would have no meaning. There would be no way of enforcing a collective
decision if persuasion failed. And what sort of conception would they
have of 'persuasion' if it were not something that could be contrasted
with giving orders?

It is clear that we are not talking about any existing society, and
that the choice between giving orders and not giving orders is not a
choice which Western society cannot take merely because of the com-
plexity of its military, economic, and political institutions, since
even in the most primitive society orders are given - if only from
parents to children. A person cannot acquire the habits of his society,
however primitive and simple, unless at some stage he has been told to.
We might, on some occasions, attempt to persuade rather than to order,
and we might devise different means of giving orders, for that is largely what politics is about. But scrapping the whole business of
giving orders can only be conceived of in a situation where there are
no conflicting interests whatever, and should such a state of affairs
come to be, where everyone sought in every respect the interests of
all, then what we would be describing would have little need for a language. It would be a society (if it could be called a society) where
nothing new could happen, where new and different ideas would not merely
fail to be accepted, but would never be thought. It would have no
future and consequently no past, no saints and no sinners, no rights
and no wrongs, no concept of individuality and no concept of society as
a whole. It would be entirely amoral and apolitical, having no literature and nothing to say. If its inhabitants did make sounds we could
never translate them since they would have no institutions similar to
our own to which we could refer as a criterion for the consistent
application of their words.

What has been argued is that a language in which no orders were given
could not be used by any conceivable way of life, and consequently it
could not qualify as an alternative language no matter how hard one
searches the imagination. If it is true that we cannot imagine a language in which orders are not given it is even less likely that we can
imagine a language consisting entirely of orders, since in that language what is to count as an order would have no other form of speech
with which one could contrast it. An order can only be an order if it
is not something else, such as an attempt to persuade, trick, appeal

to a sense of duty, loyalty, and so on. If we abstract away every other aspect of language it would not make sense to speak of a language composed entirely of orders. In fact the very concept of an order would be redundant and we would be left in the impossible situation depicted in the attempt to imagine a language without orders.

An order is something that we can agree with or disagree, approve or disapprove. How could we express our approval or disapproval in this language - by giving further orders? One usually associates living one's life according to orders with such institutions as the army. The order 'Shoot!' is only possible if one has the practice of explaining how to load and fire the rifle. One cannot tell others how to shoot by telling them to shoot. Suppose everyone were a member of the army from birth; in what sense could we speak of joining the army and submitting oneself to a life of giving and taking orders? Joining the army and submitting oneself to orders, even if conscripted, is something one can do only as an alternative to other activities. An order can only be obeyed if there exists the possibility, however remote, of disobeying it. Likewise a life composed almost entirely of order-giving and taking can only have any reality when there exists the possibility of an alternative way of life. Moreover, a society that only has a use for giving orders, and not for concepts connected with disobeying them, could not be said to have grasped the concept of 'giving orders' and therefore their language would not consist solely of giving orders in any meaningful sense. A language consisting entirely of orders could therefore be used only by a society that had no concept of what an order is, since they would never know whether what they were saying was an order. This seems to be the inherent difficulty in the attempt to imagine a language consisting entirely of orders. As soon as we imagine it, that is, abstract everything from any existing language that is not an order, then what we have imagined is not a language consisting entirely of orders.

In both the imagined languages it appears that neither versions are sound, not because they offend against the existing rules of grammar and syntax, but because if they are consistently and seriously applied we could find no conceivable way of life in which they could flourish. It must be granted that in order to know a language it is not essential to know everything about the way of life of those who speak it, but it is necessary to know something about those who use it. It is, for example, important to know whether or not it could be used by the participants in some conceivable way of life. When Hunter claims that he can imagine a language 'independently of the manner of life' he can only make this claim because he is not really imagining any genuine language at all.[15]

42

So if in the statement 'to imagine a language means to imagine a form of life', the expression 'form of life' is not equivalent to 'way of life' there is, nevertheless, a very important sense in which the imagination of a language entails the imagination of a way of life. Otherwise what would we make of: 'We could also easily imagine a language (and that means again a culture)'? (BB.134)

When Wittgenstein asks us to 'Imagine a language where...' he is not saying that this is a possible language, but simply conducting an exercise to free the philosopher from certain misconceptions about the nature of language and reality. This is the *negative* aspect of his work. Thus if he asks us to imagine a language consisting entirely of commands (PI.19), or of the words 'Block', 'Slab', or 'Stone', he is showing that languages are not the kind of things we can create arbitrarily and independently of a whole network of activities people engage in. The formula 'imagine a language where...' is, when taken in the negative sense, in many ways similar to the Hegelian advice in the Introduction to the *Phenomenology* to 'undertake the exposition of knowledge as a phenomenon', to refrain from 'making any contribution' and so on. When speaking of the objects of sensory realism Hegel tells his reader that we must present them as they appear to the realist consciousness. 'We must not...reflect and ponder about it, but only deal with it as sense certainty contains it', says Hegel. (PG.MM.83-4/B. 150-1) A contribution from us is superfluous. Sensory realism, like other philosophical positions presented in the *Phenomenology*, will reveal its own inadequacy. Hegel's intentions, like Wittgenstein's are purely descriptive. If, for example, a philosopher is bewitched by a picture of what he thinks to be the essence of language, and that essence is naming or giving commands, then the method employed by both Hegel and Wittgenstein would consist in asking him to imagine if the foundations of language were really like that. Wittgenstein described his method in terms of a battle against 'the bewitchment of our understanding through the instruments of our speech, (PI.109) and Hegel described his in terms of a 'battle of reason', which seeks to 'overcome the rigidity which the understanding has brought in'. (Enz.I.32) Both are opposed to the reification of thought which has its origin in a fascination with a one-sided picture, and the method employed to overcome this consists in returning concepts to their social context.

So far we have considered Wittgenstein's criticism of the empiricist account of language and reality. In doing so several similarities have been drawn between Wittgenstein's method of returning concepts to their social context and Hegel's method of asking the reader if human language and knowledge is acquired in the way that the empiricist model assumes. Philosophical nonsense is combatted by both Hegel and Wittgenstein by inviting the philosopher to imagine if the world is really as it is portrayed in his arguments. Can we really communicate with

gestures, however rough and ready, outside of a reasonably sophisticated cultural system? Can we really break down language and culture
into a set of atomistic practices like giving or taking orders? Could
there really be a building site where the only use of language is to
indicate a need for more building materials? Does it make sense to
speak of an essence of language whether it be naming, giving commands
or what? Is it possible for one human being to be a complete enigma
to another? Can we really deny another person is human? All of these
questions have been shown on Wittgenstein's terms to be philosophically unsound. In the following chapter we shall therefore concentrate
more directly upon Hegel's phenomenological method of revealing philosophical confusion, taking as the main text the chapter on Perception
in Hegel's *Phenomenology*.

NOTES

[1] Sartre, *Critique* Book I, Section B. pp.190-1.

[2] Ibid. p.190.

[3] Ibid. p.190.

[4] Ibid. p.190.

[5] J. F. M. Hunter, 'Forms of Life in Wittgenstein's *Philosophical
     Investigations*', in *Essays on Wittgenstein*, ed. E. D. Klemke,
     Illinois, 1971.

[6] Ibid. p.277.

[6] Ibid. p.277.

[8] Ibid. p.277.

[9] R. Rhees, 'Wittgenstein's Builders' in *Discussions of Wittgenstein*

[10] Ibid. p.71.

[11] Ibid. p.76.

[12] Hunter, op. cit, p.277.

[13] Ibid. p.277.

[14] It would be a mistake to see Hegel as a Dickensian schoolmaster,
     although he would find himself in opposition to much of contem-
     porary child psychology, just as he opposed the permissive 'play
     theory' of education, popular in his own time, on the grounds
     that it ignored the necessity of giving children an aspiration to
     grow up. (See PR.175). But Hegel's arguments have a wider appli-
     cation than the nursery. Unless one has, like the slave,
     'trembled and quaked', one will not recognise the true nature of
     bondage. The 'house nigger' of nineteenth-century America did

not see himself in bondage in the same way as the 'field nigger'. But he would have done so if his 'innermost being had trembled with fear'. (PG.MM.155/B.240) That the recognition of slavery is assisted by the lash is an important factor in the ascendency of the slave's consciousness. It requires little imagination to see how Hegel's account of fear and service, and the discipline of work, is central to Marx's account of a revolutionary class-conscious proletariat. The question 'Why did Marx choose the industrial proletariat, and not some other exploited group, as the agent of social change?' can be answered in terms of the above account of fear and service. The proletariat is essential for Marx, because it has laboured under discipline, under fear and service, and in doing so has acquired an understanding of the necessary techniques of production. It was precisely this combination of fear and service, fused into the discipline of work and combined with anger, that Marx saw as the basis for the emerging class-consciousness of the industrial proletariat.

[15] Language can only be spoken by people, and to understand a language one needs to understand people just as much as one needs to understand grammar and syntax. This is what Rhees means by: 'And it is important to emphasise, as Wittgenstein was doing, that to understand what people are saying you must understand more than vocabulary and rules of grammar. But differences between one form of life and another are not like the differences between one form of institution - say marriage customs and financial institutions - and another. And the activity of the builders does not give you the idea of a people with a definite sort of life. Do they have songs and dances and festivals and do they have legends and stories? Are they horrified by certain sorts of crimes, and do they expose people to public ridicule? The description of them on the building site, if you add, "this may be all", makes them look like marionettes. On the other hand, if they do have a life, then to say that their speaking is part of that life would be different to saying that their speaking is part of the activity of building'. *Discussions of Wittgenstein*, p.83.

45

III Perception and observation in Hegel's *Phenomenolo*

1. THE FACT-INTERPRETATION THEORY

> There is a sense, then, in which seeing is a 'theory-laden'
> undertaking. Observation of X is shaped by prior knowledge
> of X.1

> We find certain things about seeing puzzling because we do not
> find the whole business of seeing puzzling enough. [Wittgenstein,
> PI.II.xi]

One of the problems confronting Hegel's reader is that Hegel, like
Wittgenstein, gives no initial indication as to the direction of his
thought or of the nature of the problems with which he is concerned.
So rather than plunging straight into Hegel's text, it will be more
warding to consider some of the problems associated with the activit
of perception. No excuse is therefore offered for beginning a chapt
on Hegel's account of perception with a discussion of Russell, Moore
Wittgenstein, Kuhn, and Feyerabend's remarks on perception. If Hege
is worth reading at all it is because he can make a contribution to
contemporary discussion. Having thus indicated some of the problems
involved in the empiricist account of perception we shall, in the fo
lowing sections of this chapter, focus more directly upon Hegel's co
tribution to the critique of empiricist accounts of perception.

Closely bound up with realism is the assumption that there is only
one correct way of representing the world. This assumption, however
creates difficulties for the realist 'proper name theory of language
The language we speak is highly ambiguous. Russell recognised this
did not think it necessitated a drastic revision of his realist onto
logy. Instead he sought to find the closest possible fit between wo
and the world. Consider his difficulty regarding our experience of
table. According to Russell, different experiences of the table ren
different sensations:

> When in ordinary life we speak of *the* colour of the table, we
> only mean the sort of colour it will seem to have to a normal
> spectator from an ordinary point of view under usual conditions
> of light. But the other colours which appear under other con-
> ditions have just as good a right to be considered real; and
> therefore, to avoid favouritism, we are compelled to deny that,
> in itself, the table has any one particular colour.

> The same thing applies to the texture. With the naked eye
> one can see the grain, but otherwise the table looks smooth
> and even. If we looked at it through a microscope, we should
> see roughness and hills and valleys, and all sorts of
> differences that are imperceptible to the naked eye. Which

of these is the 'real' table? We are naturally tempted to say that what we see through the microscope is more real, but that in turn would be changed by a still more powerful microscope. If, then, we cannot trust what we see with the naked eye, why should we trust what we see through a microscope? Thus, again, the confidence in our senses with which we began deserts us.[2]

In the above passage Russell takes it for granted that there is only one correct way of representing things in the world; in this case the table. We are asked to 'avoid favouritism' as if there is only one correct perception of the table which, for the moment, we cannot determine. Moreover, he says that 'We are naturally tempted to say that what we see through the microscope is more real'. But is this true? The microscope is a relatively modern invention; when it was first invented it was questionable whether what was seen through it had any reality at all. Why should the microscope have any greater claim to reality than anything else? It reveals that the surface of the table is rough but this information would not prevent Russell from placing his dinner on it. To avoid the sceptical conclusions hinted at by Russell, it is necessary to point out that the word 'rough' has a different meaning in the language game of physics than it does in ordinary life. To recognise this is to allow for the possibility of speaking of different ways of representing the world. Russell's table presents him with problems because he cannot decide, without favouritism, the real meaning of the object corresponding to the word 'table'.

During the first half of the twentieth-century many philosophers sharing Russell's theory of language, but lacking his candour, have laid claim to know the correct way of representing the world with the resulting commitment to demonstrate that other accounts are mere interpretations. Others of a more sceptical bent have confessed an inability to depict the real world maintaining that we have conflicting 'interpretations' of the facts. What we shall describe as the fact-interpretation theory, that is, the belief that there is but one set of facts with many conflicting interpretations or moral evaluations, has a long ancestry in philosophy. It is the source of scepticism and positivism in both moral philosophy and epistemology, although it is not an assumption arrived at through idle speculation. However discredited this view has become in recent philosophy, it is bound up with the type of society we live in and consequently the practical applications of this philosophical assumption are an essential aspect of everyday experience. Consider, for example, a theory that is popular in Government circles: it is held that strikes and industrial unrest have their origin in a lack of communication. The assumption is that if a company's employees have the correct interpretation of all the facts they will become convinced that strikes are harmful not only to themselves but to something called 'the nation as a whole'. A few years ago a Minister of Labour made the following remarks:

> There are many aspects of our industrial life where there is
> clearly room for a great deal of improvement...one of these
> aspects is the need for good communications in industry...
> There are undoubtedly trouble-makers here and there; I think
> there always will be. But trouble-makers thrive on ignorance
> ...A well informed work-force seldom falls prey to the trouble-
> maker. Good communications cuts the ground from under his
> feet...[3]

The practical consequences of this philosophical assumption was the
formation of a 'fact-finding' Motor Industry Joint Labour Council to
tackle the problem of unofficial strikes. Its first assignment was at
the Solihull factory of the Rover company in November 1965 where it
applied the principle that if both sides of industry are presented with
the facts they will not enter into conflict. Its failure to prevent,
or even reduce, industrial unrest in the motor industry may be regarded
as a practical refutation of the fact-interpretation theory since it
can be argued that what counts as an essential fact from one side of
the industry depends on one's position in the industry.

It has been argued in the previous two chapters, that the natural
facts are not simply read off from the world, but are given in the context of a grammar which includes, and presupposes, systems of knowledge
ethical beliefs, and so on. It was maintained that there is no set of
facts existing independently of a way of life, which is essentially
what philosophers such as Hanson have in mind when they combat the fact
interpretation theory with the concept of 'theory-loaded phrases'.[4]

The philosopher depicted by Hegel as the 'Perceiving consciousness',
is in many ways similar to the Minister of Labour in the above example
Philosophically they share the same metaphysical ground as the commonsense approach associated with G. E. Moore. Whilst the Minister of
Labour held that industrial unrest could be eliminated if one concentrates upon factual descriptions Moore maintained that philosophical
perplexity could be cleared up if only one concentrates on commonsense descriptions. From the correct view that there are descriptions
of states of affairs which can be known to be ultimately correct they
leap to the false conclusion that to every state of affairs there corresponds only one correct description. This theory, however, looks
less plausible once it is realised that we can and do describe a state
of affairs correctly from a variety of points of view, using language
which varies in sophistication and theoretical load. What is meant by
'theoretical load' can be explained with reference to the following
examples.[5]

a. A doctor inspecting a mark on a man's face, sees it as a scar
    and describes it as such.

b. A fourteenth-century peasant, inspecting a mark on a man's face,
    sees it as a mark of the devil, and describes it as such.

Now when the doctor describes what he sees as a scar an element of
theory is already built into the description. He knows, for instance,
that it was caused by a wound, a wound that was serious. He must know
that it was not caused by a surgeon's knife, since no surgeon would
make a jagged incision. Perceiving it as a scar he reveals his knowledge about the nature of the wound, and this presupposes an acquaintance with a considerable body of modern medicine. Scars have not
always been associated with wounds, but nowadays the terms 'scar' and
'wound' belong to the same grammar. In the same way the fourteenth-
century peasant, who sees a mark of the devil, is bringing to the act
of perception, a whole dimension of religion, superstition, and the
culture appropriate to his historical epoch.

But are they not merely seeing the same facts, imposing on them
widely divergent interpretations? No. There is no way in which we can
find a theory-neutral description that will satisfy both the doctor and
the peasant. To commit the doctor to some allegedly neutral description, say 'skin mark', would be to denigrate the whole body of knowledge upon which his proficiency depends. We might say that too much
of modern medicine hangs on the relationship between wounds and scars
for it to be relegated to the realm of contingency. In a similar way
committing the peasant to some neutral terminology would entail a deni-
gration of his religious world-view.

Let us now examine this example in Hegel's terms. According to Hegel
the doctor's experience of the scar is mediated by his knowledge of
medicine, his past training and the culture in which he has developed
his skills. The peasant's immediate recognition of the mark of the
devil is likewise mediated by his religious belief. For Hegel, any
claim to perceptual knowledge with any degree of determinateness must
be mediated, at least by an antithesis of what it is not, but primarily
by the system in which the perception is made. As the system develops
what was formerly mediated becomes immediate. In the case of the
doctor his recognition of the scar is immediate. Yet in another - a
more elementary-sense his initial recognition of the scar is mediated
by his knowledge and training in medicine - as opposed to witchcraft,
of which he has no system of mediations.

Hegel's point is that at different levels of knowledge different
facts are undisputed. Certain things are taken as immediate data, even
though at another level their very recognition is mediated. For

example, what is the result of a difficult calculation to a child is
often immediate to an adult. Yet this does not mean that the adult's
inference is immediate in the sense of being without any system of
mediations. There is no item of knowledge that is purely or absolutely
immediate. This assumption was the reef upon which the standpoint of
sense-certainty was wrecked, and is a recurring theme in the
Phenomenology.

The Perceiver, like the sensory realist, assumes that the facts are
independent of the various systems of mediations in which they are presented. Thus a rigid distinction between fact and interpretation is
generated out of the existence of conflicting descriptions. If there
is only one set of facts then conflict can only arise over the way they
are interpreted. This assumption lies behind the traditional account
of dispute within the sciences. Conflicting theories have been explained in terms of 'better' or 'worse' interpretations of the facts.
To break the hold of this picture it is necessary to refer to an example from the history of science. For many years it has been held
that Galileo had discovered certain facts with the aid of his telescope
which the Aristotelians had either ignored or refused to accept for
dogmatic reasons. Recently it has been argued that the Aristotelians
did have a genuine case against Galileo. By what right did Galileo
raise his telescope to the status of a superior sense? P. K. Feyerabend, for example, points out that when Galileo brought his telescope
to the house of his opponent, Magini, in Bologna, on the night of
April 24-5, 1610, not one of the twenty-four professors present saw the
new planets (the moons of Jupiter) distinctly. Why were they incapable
of seeing the 'facts' before their eyes? Says Feyerabend:

> Today we understand a little better why the direct appeal to
> telescopic vision was bound to lead to disappointment, especially
> in the initial stages. The main reason, one already forseen
> by Aristotle, was, of course, the fact that the senses applied
> under abnormal conditions are liable to give an abnormal res-
> ponse. Some of the older historians had an inkling of the
> situation, but they speak *negatively*; they try to explain the
> absence of satisfactory observational reports, the poverty of
> what is seen in the telescope. They are unaware of the possi-
> bility that the observers might have been disturbed by *strong
> positive illusions* also. The extent of such illusions was not
> realised until recently, mainly as the result of the work of
> Ronchi and his school. Here the greatest variations are re-
> ported in the placement of the telescopic image and, corres-
> pondingly, in the observed magnification. Some observers put
> the image right inside the telescope, making it change its
> lateral position with the lateral position of the eye, exactly
> as would be the case with an after image or a reflex inside the

50

telescope - an excellent proof that one must be dealing with an 'illusion'. Others place the image in a manner that leads to no magnification at all, although a linear magnification of over thirty may have been promised. Even a doubling of images can be explained as the result of a lack of proper focusing. Adding to those psychological difficulties the many imperfections of the contemporary telescopes, one not only can well understand the scarcity of satisfactory reports, but is astonished at the speed with which the reality of the new phenomena was accepted and, as was the custom, publicly acknowledged. This development becomes even more puzzling when we consider that many reports of even the best observers were either plainly false, and capable of being shown as such at the time, or else self-contradictory.[6]

Feyerabend concludes that:

Galileo had only slight acquaintance with contemporary optical theory. His telescope gave surprising results on the earth and these were duly praised. However, trouble was to be expected in the sky, as we know now. Trouble promptly arose: the telescope produced spurious and contradictory phenomena, and some of its results could be refuted by a single look with the unaided eye. Only a new theory of telescopic vision could possibly bring order into the chaos (which may have been still larger, due to the different phenomena seen at the time even with the naked eye) and separate appearance from reality. Such a theory was developed by Kepler, first in 1604 and then again in 1611.[7]

The appeal to perception, to the evidence of the eyes, in the above example, was unsatisfactory largely because of the unfamiliarity with the telescope. The 'proof' of Galileo's theory could not be determined solely by looking through the telescope, it was necessary to convince people that what they were looking at was the correct data. The image in the telescope is not obvious, a considerable theoretical contribution is necessary. The point is that different theoretical frameworks produce different sensory phenomena.[8] On the other hand, the empiricist is committed to the view that there is only one set of facts independent of the theoretical framework. Conflicting accounts of the facts are dismissed as illusory (encouraging a sceptical tendency) or as incorrect interpretations. But is the activity of seeing really a matter of interpreting facts this way or that? In his analysis of 'seeing as' (PI.II.xi) Wittgenstein introduces the concept of 'seeing under an aspect', which involves neither the interpretation of facts in various ways nor the perceiving of a change in the properties of the object experienced. For example, when looking at gestalt-switch pictures like the 'duck-rabbit' drawing I can say: 'Now I see it as a duck', and later 'Now I can see it as a rabbit'. But to what change am I referring? I cannot describe this alteration. What is being described is a different visual experience.

> The change of aspect. 'But surely you would say that the picture is altogether different now!'
> But what is different: my impression my point of view? - Can I say? I *describe* the alteration like a perception: quite as if the object had altered before my eyes.
> 'Now I am seeing *this*', I might say (pointing to another picture, for example). This has the form of a report of a new perception.
> The expression of a change of aspect is the expression of a *new* perception and at the same time of the perception's being unchanged. (PI.II.xi)

So the answer to the question 'Have different properties been perceived when it was seen as a duck and then as a rabbit?' is that what is reported on each occasion is a complete description. And if it is claimed that what I see is a certain visual image which can be interpreted this way or that, then it is proper to ask what kind of an interpretation is being talked about here? We can speak of being halfway through an interpretation but not halfway through seeing a diagram as a rabbit or a duck. Seeing something as a rabbit is not the same as interpreting something as a rabbit - if indeed there is any context in which we could speak meaningfully of interpreting something as a rabbit. An interpretation can be false; it can also be corrected or improved. In what sense could we correct or improve the visual experience of seeing something as a rabbit?

It might be objected that the kind of interpretation we impose on the facts is not the same kind of activity as that which takes place when we are said to be interpreting a dream. Perhaps when we 'interpret' the duck-rabbit this way or that or the scar, in the above-mentioned example, we make an instant interpretation; too instant for observation. But what is an instant interpretation? Do we instantly interpret the objects we eat with as knives and forks? 'Instantaneous interpretation, says Hanson, 'hails from that limbo that produced unsensed sensibilia, unconscious inference, incorrigible statements, negative facts and objective. These are ideas which philosophers force on the world to preserve some pet epistemological or metaphysical theory'.[9]

One of the assumptions behind the fact-interpretation theory is the realist belief that what I really see is produced in me by the object. In the case of the duck-rabbit this is clearly not the case since it i possible for me to reproduce exactly what I am seeing when I see it as a rabbit, whilst another may see this reproduction as a duck. Nor is the solipsistic idealist alternative an improvement, since I cannot describe the action of the senses which caused an alternation between seeing it as a duck and seeing it as a rabbit. The shifting glance belongs no more to the ego than to the object. What we have when we see something first as a duck and then as a rabbit are two distinct visual experiences.

> Do I really see something different each time, or do I only interpret what I see differently in a different way? I am inclined to say the former. But why? - To interpret is to think, to do something; seeing is a state. (PI.II.xi)

In the example of the scar - mark of the devil,each perceiver experiences according to the way of life in which they are active participants. The question whether they interpret the same facts differently or experience different facts does not arise. What is going on are two distinct activities: either you see it as a scar or as a mark of the devil, in which case you bring your knowledge to the experience. There is no fact independent of the means of taking hold of it.

The perceiving consciousness, depicted by Hegel, does not hold this view. As we shall see, in the following section, he believes that the world consists of an independent realm of properties sensuously given. If we are to be true to Hegel's descriptive method, we must therefore adopt the posture of one who gives an account of our perception of the world according to this assumption.

2. TAKING THE STANDPOINT OF PERCEPTION SERIOUSLY

> ...if physics were based solely on perception, and perceptions were nothing more than the evidence of the senses, then the physical act would consist only in seeing, hearing, smelling, etc., and animals, too, would be in this way physicists. But what sees, hears, etc., is a Mind, a thinker. (Enz.II.246zu)

In the chapter on perception in the *Phenomenology* Hegel further develops his discussion of the difficulties inherent in empiricism. From sensory realism, and its preoccupation with the objects of sense as the foundation of human knowledge, Hegel turns to a more sophisticated version of realism, which he characterises as 'Perception'. The title of this chapter signifies a typical Hegelian pun: *Warhnehmung*, which literally means 'to take truly', implies taking truly that which is given in sense experience. In an even deeper sense it reflects one of the guiding principles of Hegel's phenomenological method: to take truly, or seriously, that which appears in the works of the philosopher throughout the history of philosophy. In this chapter Hegel's target is the materialism of commonsense, normally put forward as an antidote to philosophical speculation. Hegel rejects this view, insisting that commonsense is a 'good substitute for real philosophy in the way that chicory is lauded as a good substitute for coffee'. (PG.MM.63/B.126)

From the standpoint of perception the question is: Should we regard the perceiver as playing a major or a minor part in the activity of perception? Should we analyse perception in terms of the subject or the object of perception? Does the object's being depend on it being perceived? Or does it exist independently of our experience of it, independently of our methods of classifying the objects in the natural world, our culture, way of life and systems of mediations? In other words are the qualities of objects naturally given to a passive subject The tension Hegel uncovers, when he depicts perception as the 'taking truly of the sensuously given', is between perception-as-passive-reception and perception-as-an-act-of-knowledge.

Whereas the standpoint of sense-certainty is faced with the choice between self-contradiction and solipsistic silence the domain of *Wahrnehmung* is a public one. Unlike sense data, percepts are describable in terms of perceivably determinate properties. Perceiving, here in depicted, is characterised in terms of a relationship between a subject that passively receives and an object that is perceived. But what is significant about this standpoint is the view that the object, with its properties, does have an existence independently of the means of classifying phenomena. From this standpoint, however, the truth lies in the object; it matters little whether it is perceived, the act of perceiving being what Hegel depicts as a 'non-essential moment'.

So what, asks Hegel, is this object confronting the Perceiver? According to the assumptions of commonsense realism the Perceiver 'takes truly' what is perceived and passively receives what is given in experience. Hegel's approach consists in asking the Perceiver-philosopher to demonstrate his ability to passively record the given object - in this case a cube of salt - as a thing endowed with determinate properties since, according to the Perceiver, 'the object shows itself by so doing to be a *thing with many properties*'. (PG.MM.94/B.162) What is seen is sense-dependent, but what the senses reveal are universally recognisable properties.

> The sense element is in this way itself still present, but not
> in the form of some particular that is 'meant' - as had to be
> in the case of immediate certainty - but as a universal, as that
> which will have the character of a *property*. (PG.MM.94/B.163)

But, asks Hegel, given that we perceive universal properties and not particular unrelated sense-impressions, are we any better off than the standpoint of sense-certainty? Unless we know something over and above these properties we could not understand which properties belong to the object and which do not; we would lack a principle of classification. These universal properties, then, being 'self-related, are indifferent to each other, each is by itself free from the rest...they inter-penetrate without affecting one another'. (PG.MM.94-5/B.164) As such, the universal qualities perceived are themselves abstractions, which Hegel characterises as 'Thinghood' (*Dingheit*), and are 'nothing else than the Here and Now as this on analysis turned out to be, viz., a simple to-getherness of many Heres and Nows'. (PG.MM.95/B.164)

Hegel's treatment of the perceiving standpoint is therefore similar to that of his treatment of sense-certainty. He asks the Perceiver the following question: "Here is a piece of salt", he says, "but you cannot call it a piece of salt since, according to you, it is merely a collection of universal qualities which, as you say, 'do not affect each other in their inter-penetration'. There are before you the properties of whiteness, tartness of taste, and cubical shape. But you, who recognise these universal properties, must tell me what principle you employ to unite these manifold distinct properties in one object. Moreover, if as you say, the 'many determinate properties are utterly indifferent to each other, and are entirely related to themselves alone', they would not be determinate; for they are so, merely in so far as they are *distinguished* and related to others as opposites". (PG.MM.95 /B.165) In other words, we cannot learn of properties in isolation from other items of knowledge. To recognise a property involves, amongst other things, knowing how to recognise what it is not. This is essentially Geach's point when he argues that knowing the concept 'red' is bound up with knowing what is not red; that there is not another realm of negative facts - as Russell and the naive realists thought - which can be learnt in addition to the 'facts' standing in immediate relationship to the senses. As Geach says, "Surely what I exercise in using the term 'not red' is simply the concept *red*; knowing what *is* red and knowing what *is not* red are inseparable - *eadem est scientia opposito-rum*".[10]

If someone claims to have knowledge of an object by virtue of its properties he must also know something about the properties it does not have. Of course these properties are not given in the immediacy of perception. It follows that to say anything about a thing one must go beyond the actual perception of its properties. But such complexities fall outside of the simple consciousness depicted in the present phenomenal standpoint. At the root of the Perceiver's difficulty is the assumption that perception is passive and its object is something independent, an assumption common to traditional empiricist thought.

But for a percept to possess determinate properties in its own right it must possess properties which are not given in passive perception, since only in the possession of them can it enjoy independence. This, as it will be argued, is the paradox of the Perceiver's standpoint. However, we, who must imitate the standpoint of the Perceiver, must assume that our knowledge of a thing and its properties is exactly as the Perceiver tells us.

Given Hegel's method, what is the criterion for deciding whether the reported perceptions are correct? If the object, on this view, is 'true and universal' then might it not be the case that 'consciousness apprehends the object wrongly and deceives itself'? (PG.MM.97/B.167) Hegel allows the Perceiver to be aware of this possibility, but points out that his only possible criterion could be 'self-sameness', and that as the data before him is diverse the procedure will consist of 'relating the diverse moments of his apprehension to one another' in a simple one to one correlation. (PG.MM.97/B.167) However, we should note that because this standpoint assumes the object to be true and independent of our ways of classifying it the responsibility for the failure to match two experiences together would lie with the Perceiver and not the object. It is in this way that the area of interest in Hegel's *Gedanken experimente* falls upon the Perceiver rather than the object of his apprehension.

Hegel puts the following question to the Perceiver: 'what sort of experience does consciousness form in the course of its actual perception'? (PG.MM.97/B.167) What kind of experience is this passive reception of sensory qualities? "The object, which is apprehended, presents itself as purely 'one' and single", replies the Perceiver. "Moreover I am aware of the 'property' (*Eigenschaft*) in it, a property which is universal, thereby transcending the particularity of the object. The first form of being, in which the objective reality has the sense of a 'one', and thus was not its true being; and since the *object* is the true fact here, the untruth falls on my side, and the apprehension was not correct. According to my account of the universality of the property I am therefore required to take the objective entity as a community (*Gemeinschaft*) of properties". (PG.MM.97/B.167) This is the contradictory standpoint of the perceiving consciousness; the object is perceived as both one and many.

So the question we must now put to the Perceiver is 'Is the object perceived one or many?' Are we to consider it as a community of properties or as one thing? What is the principle one employs to unite these properties into one object? If these properties are universal and could belong to any object how do we know that they belong to this object - this cube of salt - before us? How do we know that the tartness of taste, cubical shape, and whiteness before us belong to one

56

object and to nothing else? Normally of course, we would not ask these questions, but it does make sense to ask them of a philosopher who maintains that the activity of perception involves nothing more than the passive awareness of properties sensuously given. One might think that the One-Many argument that Hegel is employing is not a satisfactory refutation of the Perceiver's standpoint. It is obviously not, but then Hegel's method is to present the problems as they occur within the standpoint he is depicting. For this reason Hegel's employment of a sceptical argument of this nature is justified as a short-term measure. The Perceiver's dilemma is: whether to say the thing is one and deny the universality of its properties, holding that they can only belong to this cube of salt, or to assert the universality of its properties and deny that the thing is one? According to Hegel the Perceiver reacts to this dilemma by falling back on the claim that all we see are atomic properties; that the given object is experienced as a plurality of properties. But this position abandons the perceptual standpoint, for now the Perceiver cannot maintain his claim to perceive a concrete object before him, experiencing only a set of disconnected properties. The position forced on him is that of sense-certainty.

3. CRITICAL REALISM

What a man sees depends both upon what he looks at and also upon what his previous visual-conceptual experience has taught him to see. In the absence of such training there can only be, in William James's phrase, 'a bloomin' buzzin' confusion.[11]

The question is: should the Perceiver return to the standpoint of sense-certainty or revise the standpoint of Perception? In fact a return to sense-certainty is ruled out since there is no point in maintaining a discussion with one who retreats to a position that has already been examined and found wanting. On the strength of this dilemma the dialectic moves forward, though it should not be forgotten that we are still dealing with the basic assumptions of traditional empiricism and the object-receptor theory of knowledge.

Seeing the above-mentioned dilemma from the standpoint of the Perceiver, it appears that the latter is aware that he does perceive one object, but the 'evidence of his senses' commits him to the assertion that what is seen is a community of properties. He therefore resorts to a subjective appeal, a 'return back into consciousness', in which he says 'I am aware of the thing as a one, but, if in the course of my perceiving something crops up contradicting that then I must take it to be due to my reflection'. (PG.MM.99/B.169) That is to say, perceiving the object as a many is due to the diversity of the sense-organs; this solitary cube of salt is in point of fact, 'merely white to our eyes, also tart to our tongue, and also cubical to our feeling, and so on'. (PG.MM.99/B.170) With this line of reasoning we can conclude that the object's diversity comes not from the thing, but from the sense organs of the Perceiver. The distinctness of the sense organs entails that the perception of the object will be of its diverse properties. So whilst the Perceiver 'knows' the thing to be one, his sense-experience is of its many properties. Hence: 'We are consequently, the universa medium where such elements get disassociated, and exist each by itself' (PG.MM.99/B.170) The thing is one, but insofar as it is perceived by the senses it is many. On the other hand the one-ness of the object i determined by the unifying process of the mind: "Putting these pro- perties into a 'one' belongs solely to consciousness", says the Percei ver. (PG.MM.101/B.171)

It is in this way that the Perceiver admits that the object's plura- lity and singularity is determined by himself. The transference of th many properties of the thing to the unifying mind re-establishes the thing's unity and 'self-sameness'. The unifying mind supersedes the disparate sensory properties. What is wrong with this picture? In th first place it is held that the salt is objective because its qualitie are objective. What is subjective is the activity of the mind in the uniting of these qualities into a single entity. We do not have a cri terion for determining whether the object is one; all that has been argued so far is that consciousness holds the properties together. Bu given that the mind unites them, why should the salt, in itself, be a unity any more than a plurality? Which is more important? And what i the criterion according to which the mind determines the unity or plurality of phenomena? The mind can either unite or separate them with equal plausibility. By what principle does the mind unite the qualities of whiteness, tartness, etc., into a single cube of salt?

Now being of equal plausibility these two alternatives entail a thir possibility; if the operation of the mind can reveal divergent results the thing must be capable of adapting itself to antithetical categorie For instance: 'Now I see it as a many, now I see it as a one', just a we can say with the duck-rabbit 'Now I see it as a duck, now a rabbit' From the standpoint of Wahrnehmung (taking truly the information of th senses) if the senses reveal antithetical categories then the object must possess antithetical properties and is capable of changing from a one to a many. Because the Perceiver can alternatively attribute the object's singularity and plurality to himself he must also view the object as exhibiting two contradictory modes of being. Otherwise he would be committed to an explanation of how the thing appears indepen- dently of actual perception, a position which supersedes that of Perception.[12] The position which the Perceiver finds himself obliged to accept is that:

Consciousness thus finds through this comparison that not only *its* way of taking the truth contains the diverse moments of apprehension and return upon itself, but that the truth itself, the thing, manifests itself in this twofold moment. (PG.MM.101/B.172)

If the object is given in this twofold manner the Perceiver must abandon the idea that the mind is the source of the object's unity or plurality. In this way the experiment with critical realism returns once more to the naive realism of sense-certainty.

The Perceiver's claim to alternate between seeing the object as one or a many has certain affinities with the point expressed in Wittgenstein's example of the duck-rabbit in the *Investigations* II.xi. When considering the report 'Now it is a duck, now it is a rabbit' it is possible to draw two conclusions. We may (i) think that we are interpreting the same data differently, or (ii) think that the object must be changing. But Wittgenstein argues 'seeing as' involves (i) no difference of interpretation, and (ii) no change in the properties of the object, but merely seeing under a different aspect. This, of course, involves a more active consciousness than the perceiving consciousness. The same argument can be applied to the Perceiver's account of the object's plurality and singularity. 'Now I see it as a one, now I see it as a many' does not involve any change in the object or the perceptual apparatus.

Wittgenstein's point is that seeing implies a grammar and a considerable exercise of the imagination. For example to see this triangle

as an object that has fallen over, says Wittgenstein, 'demands imagination'.(PI.II.xi) Similarly he asks, 'Doesn't it take imagination to hear something as a variation on a particular theme? And yet one is perceiving something in so hearing it'. (PI.II.xi)

Wittgenstein's argument here can shed light upon Hegel's treatment of the perceiving consciousness. Both Hegel and Wittgenstein are anxious to stress the internal link between seeing and thinking. Says Wittgenstein:

Is it a question of both seeing *and* thinking? or an amalgam of the two, as I should almost like to say? (PI.II.xi)

And

It is almost as if 'seeing the sign in this context' were an
echo of a thought. 'The echo of a thought in sight' - one
would like to say. (PI.II.xi)[13]

The point is that there is more to perception than the exercise of the
relevant sense organs. Wittgenstein, like Hegel, is anxious to draw
attention to the internal relation between the present the past and
other objects with the object of perception. For example:

I meet someone whom I have not seen for years; I see him
clearly, but fail to know him. Suddenly I know him, I see
the old face in the altered one. (PI.II.xi)

In the above example the 'dawning of an aspect' did not involve any
change in the visual data; instead a connection was made between the
present experience and previous ones. This is why Wittgenstein says t
'what I perceive in the dawning of an aspect is...an internal relation
between it (the object) and other objects'. (PI.II.xi) But according
to the Perceiver there is no employment or contribution of knowledge t
the act of perception. The Perceiver claims to receive sense-impressions which are assembled into a plurality or a singularity without an
contribution other than the senses and the unifying operation of the
mind. For that reason, if he is faced with contradictory accounts of
an experience, or changing aspects, he must either assert that the
structure of the object is changeable or the senses are deceptive.

4. SUMMARY

We may summarise the previous two sections by saying that in section 2
the Perceiver was forced to admit that perception and reception were
not equal, and his failure to provide an account of the interdependent
of properties returned him to the standpoint of sense-certainty. On
the other hand the vain attempt in section 3 to introduce reflection a
an intervening medium entailed the assertion that the thing is what
the Perceiver takes it to be after allowing for the contribution of th
unifying mind. But the difficulty with this standpoint was the inability to indicate exactly what the mind should take upon itself. The
Perceiver claimed on the one hand that the unitary character of the
thing was subjective, whilst on the other hand he held that, owing to
the primacy of the sense organs, the plurality of the object was also
subjectively determined. The outcome of this *Gedankenexperimente* lef
the Perceiver in a further impasse: by allocating contradictory func
tions to the knowing subject he bestowed contradictory aspects upon th
object. A return to the anomalous standpoint of sense-certainty can
only be averted by a further attempt to bolster up the perceiving
standpoint.

5. SOPHISTICATED COMMONSENSE: THE SOPHISTRY OF 'INSOFAR AS'

> What would a Roman or a Greek make of a jet plane, or a radio?
> Or coming down to the simple things, if you saw a slab of
> chocolate for the first time you might think it was for
> mending shoes, lighting the fire, or building houses - about
> the last thing you'd think was that that hard brown rectangle
> was meant for eating - and when you did find that out, you'd
> most likely try eating soap too, because the texture was
> similar and the colour more attractive.[14]

This new position represents an attempt to have it both ways; to maintain the advantages of naive realism from one point of view and the advantages of critical realism from another standpoint. In Hegel's terms, the object of this consciousness 'is now the entire process which was previously shared between the object and consciousness'. (PG.MM. 101/B.172) The Perceiver, on this standpoint, however, becomes a prey for sophistry, betraying himself with his reliance upon the qualifying expression 'insofar as'. The thing is held to be one 'insofar as it is for itself' and not 'for another'. In other words, the object is whatever it becomes by virtue of its various relations. For example, 'insofar as it is influenced by this...it will exhibit qualities differing from those when it is taken by itself'. Crucial here is the fatuous qualification 'It all depends on...' A thing is held to have no fixed status; what is perceived is relative to different points of view. The cube of salt, according to this argument, would have one set of qualities insofar as it is seen from this aspect, and another set of qualities insofar as it is seen from another aspect.

The standpoint of 'Sophisticated Commonsense' might be expressed thus: unity and diversity belong to the thing perceived, but in no absolute fashion. A thing is one insofar as I focus my attention on it, but insofar as I shift my gaze to its many properties I alter my perspective and view it as a medium of disparate universals. The 'sophistry of insofar as' seeks, in this way, to render the contradiction between the one and the many innocuous. For example:

> The thing is, thus, doubtless as it stands (*an und für sich*)
> selfsame, but this unity with itself is disturbed by other
> things. In this way the unity of the thing is preserved, and,
> at the same time, the otherness is preserved outside the thing
> as well as outside consciousness. (PG.MM.102/B.173)

Of course this position does express a certain truth, but grasping what is true in this picture involves considerable knowledge and informed discrimination, not the sensation-based opinion of the Perceiver. To see something as a duck or a rabbit or a fallen triangle, requires considerable knowledge and imagination, but the question Hegel is raising here goes deeper than that which is answered by indicating the imaginations's ability to see something as something. One might, with the aid of the imagination, see the duck-rabbit as either a duck or a rabbit, but this is not similar to seeing a cube of salt as either a solitary cube or a manifold of unrelated properties. We do not, for example, speak of seeing something as either a cube of salt (with the possible exception of a discussion about artistic representation) or a manifold of unrelated properties. Seeing a cube of salt is not a mere exercise of the imagination on a par with the ability to see eithe a duck or a rabbit in a picture. To treat both examples as similar is, according to Hegel, to commit oneself to the position of extreme re-lativism depicted as the 'sophistry of insofar as'.

There are, of course, severe limitations on Wittgenstein's model of 'seeing as', which is why it should only be employed as an initial step towards breaking the hold of the fact-interpretation theory. For ex-ample, if someone speaks of seeing something as something it is always possible to ask 'What is it that is seen as something?' In this way we fall into the Kantian problem of the unknowable thing in itself. To see something as something actually presupposes a neutral fact, the 'thing' independently of how we see it. The duck-rabbit sketch, is suc a neutral thing, it is Jastrow's famous duck-rabbit. It is a standard example in psychology, a drawing which can be seen this way or that according to one's gestalt. Similarly the example of the fallen triang is a drawing on a page which can be seen this way or that. There is, nevertheless, something objective on the page to which we can switch our gestalts. But these types of gestalt switches do not take place with regard to real objects. If we are confronted with a fallen tree across the road we do not see it *as* a fallen tree, we *see* a fallen tre What else could we see it as? Drawing attention to gestalt switches is only helpful in making an inroad into the fact-interpretation theory. Kuhn, for example, recognizes both the limitations and the value of gestalt switch models. Speaking of 'paradigm' switches he remarks how:

> Others who have noted this aspect of scientific advance have emphasised its similarity to a change in visual gestalt: the marks on paper that were first seen as a bird are now seen as an antelope and vice-versa. That parallel can be misleading. Scientists do not see something *as* something else; instead they simply see it...Nevertheless, the switch of gestalt, particular because it is today so familiar, is a useful ele-mentary prototype for what occurs in full-scale paradigm shift.15

Whilst an exchange of conceptual frameworks, or in Hegel's terms a tra ition from one shape (gestalt) of consciouness to another, resembles the prototype of 'seeing as', in neither science nor everyday life is it po to switch backwards and forwards from one to another. No scientist wou conceive of switching backwards and forwards from phlogiston theory. It is similar with the conceptual switch accompanying the Copernican revolution. Says Kuhn:

> Looking at the moon, the convert to Copernicanism does not say, 'I used to see a planet, but now I see a satellite'. That locution would imply a sense in which the Ptolemaic system had once been correct. Instead, a convert to the new astronomy says, 'I once took the moon to be (or saw the moon as) a planet, but I was mistaken'. That sort of statement does recur in the aftermath of scientific revolutions.16

A change of paradigms, or shapes, involves a commitment to a different conceptual framework which is hard to reverse.

> Lavoisier...saw oxygen where Priestley had seen dephlogisticated air and where others had seen nothing at all. In learning to see oxygen, however, Lavoisier also had to change his view on many other more familiar substances...as a result of discovering oxygen, Lavoisier saw nature differently...after discovering oxygen Lavoisier worked in a different world.17

Having made the switch it is not possible to return to the previous position without rejecting that very commitment to the new paradigm that made the initial switch possible.

Returning to Hegel's example concerning the cube of salt it is now apparent why we cannot switch from seeing it as a cube to seeing it as a manifold of properties. In order to see a manifold of properties it would be necessary to belong to a different way of life, to live, as Kuhn suggests, in a different world, one in which there was a point in organising the world differently. Such a world would then exist in which different visual experiences would present themselves to someone confronted with what in our world is a cube of salt. This world would be radically different from the present and the adoption of its practices would not be a reversible choice: it would be a commitment to a set of practices radically different to those known at present. To be able to alternate between seeing something as a cube of salt and seeing it as a manifold of properties, one would need to live in a world where this difference was relatively unimportant. Only under such circumstances could we speak of seeing it as a cube of salt, since the possibility of conflicting accounts would make sense. But in the present world the claim to see it as a cube of salt must be countered with the question 'What else could it possibly be?' What is the point of classifying it as something else? We cannot adopt such a new set of conventions for classifying the world without committing ourselves to a full-scale rejection of most of our existing practices.

However, the perceiving consciousness has no concern with paradigms, gestalts, or conceptual frameworks; he is simply trying to describe the properties before him insofar as he chooses to see this or that aspect. In accord with Hegel's advice we (the phenomenological observers) must make no contribution and, refraining from all talk of paradigms and conceptual frameworks, immerse ourselves in the standpoint of the Perceiver. Standing in the same ground as the Perceiver, Hegel puts the following question to him: if it is merely a question of how one chooses to see the cube of salt then suppose we decide to see it as a unity and therefore ignore its manifold relationships, what then? Suppose the Perceiver isolates, for exclusive notice, a single object, disregarding its relationships; how can he speak of its perceived unity? A thing can enjoy distinction only when it is differentiated from other things. But things cannot be differentiated apart from their properties and since properties are universal, the lack of a criterion for their unification reappears to plague the assumption of a perceived unity. The Perceiver must therefore introduce a qualification into his account. Hegel depicts him introducing a distinction between 'essential and inessential properties'. The recognition of the former, it is claimed, serves as a criterion for the perception of the object's unity. In this way the 'determinate characteristic, which constitutes the essential character of the thing and distinguishes it from all others, is now so defined that thereby the thing stands in opposition to others, but must therein preserve itself for itself, (*für sich*)'. (PG.MM.103/B.174)

This qualification, however, exposes further anomalies in the Perceiver's standpoint. Suppose we, taking the Perceiver seriously, attempt to fasten our attention upon the object's essential property, ignoring all others, how do we then decide what this essential property is? Does this activity render all other properties inessential? Consider the Perceiver's position. He has attempted to isolate a thing by virtue of its essential nature, but the very act of picking out the essential property implicitly reveals that attention has been focused upon other properties outside the immediate field of sensory experience. For example, if he fastens on the salt's whiteness he is invoking a grammar of colour concepts, which are excluded. The attempt to perceive the true nature of a thing by fastening on the perception of its essential nature is ultimately doomed for the very reason that a thing can be essentially itself only if it can be explicitly distinguished from other things.

But what if singularity itself appears to be the essentially determinate property? Hegel is prepared for this objection since he has already argued that exclusiveness is entirely dependent upon otherness. There can be no perception of a thing in its absolute independence:

It is, however, a thing, a self-existent 'one', only so far
as it does not stand in relation to others. For in this relation, the connection with another is rather the point emphasised, and connection with another means giving up self-
existence, means ceasing to have a being on its own account.
It is precisely through the absolute character and its opposition that the thing relates itself to others, and is
essentially this process of relation, and only this. The
relation, however, is the negation of its independence, and
the thing collapses through its own essential property.
(PG.MM.102/B.174)

In the forefront of Hegel's mind is the view that logical relations
have a certain priority over sensory perception. We can bring this out
with reference to Wittgenstein's remarks concerning logical relations,
which are to be found in the *Tractatus*. According to Wittgenstein we
do not acquire a knowledge of objects by passive perception but on the
contrary:

If I know an object, I also know all its possible occurrences
in states of affairs. (Every one of these possibilities must
be part of the nature of the object). A new possibility cannot be discovered later. (TLP.2.0123)

A knowledge of the 'nature of the object' is not knowledge by acquaintance. To know the nature of an object is to know its internal properties, those properties which an object must possess, properties
which it is unthinkable that it should not possess. As Wittgenstein
says:

A property is internal if it is unthinkable that its object
should not possess it. (TLP.4.123)
If I am to know an object, though I need not know its external properties, I must know all its internal properties.
(TLP.2.01231)

An internal property of a pencil would be its dimension, whereas an external property of a pencil would be its specific colour. If we did
not know its internal properties we could not be said to know the object in any sense, whereas a knowledge of its external properties is
inessential. Knowledge of an object's internal properties is a conceptual matter. There are properties, for example, that one cannot
conceive of a pencil possessing, such as honesty, kindness, intelligence, and so on. Both Hegel and Wittgenstein would find themselves in
agreement with the view that unless some conceptual knowledge precedes
experience we cannot make a primary identification of the object, since
we would lack a knowledge of the relevant properties that one identifies

65

it with. A knowledge of an object's internal (conceptual) properties is necessary for any meaningful perceptual experience. One may acquire a knowledge of its external properties, such as colour, by looking, but a knowledge of the internal properties is logically prior to sense-experience. One does not look at a pencil to see whether it has a size or a colour, as one does to determine the exactitude of its size or colour.

If one operates with the realist ontology held by the Perceiver, there is no conceptual difference between internal and external properties, since the former are assumed to be more properties of the same kind. Like Wittgenstein, Hegel maintains this distinction and recognises that the perceiving consciousness does not. This is why the latter cannot meet Hegel's challenge to individuate a cube of salt from a multiplicity of perceptual sensations.

The gist of the above argument is that we cannot perceive uniquely. An act of perception must take in the additional relations and properties that are excluded from the sensory experience. There is more to seeing than mere looking, than the mere exercise of the senses. Hegel stresses this point when he says that: 'sensible singleness thus disappears in the dialectic process of immediate certainty and becomes universality', but merely sensuous universality, since the role of the intelligence in the act of perception has not yet been introduced. (PG. MM.104/B.176) For this reason Hegel concludes the dialogue with the Perceiver with a timely polemic against the appeal to commonsense, thus combining a criticism of his contemporaries with his analysis of the empiricist standpoint.

The appeal to commonsense in its philosophical guise, says Hegel, is responsible for the tension between unity and plurality which bedevilled the Perceiver's standpoint. In order to avoid the contradictions built into the assumption of perception-as-reception the Perceiver sought refuge behind a cloak of sophistry. The object was held to be one insofar as it was seen as one, but many insofar as it was seen as many. When this failed to provide an adequate account of the object an equally fatuous attempt was made to identify the object in terms of its essential property. But the essential, or internal, properties of objects are not determined by sensuous perception but by what Wittgenstein would call the 'grammatical rules'; and these precede sense-perception.

The ultimate irony behind the Sophistry of Commonsense is that, from the standpoint of commonsense, it is the philosopher who is criticised for his use of abstractions. Yet on examination the objects of sense are as equally vacuous as the alleged abstract objects of thought which are held to occupy the philosopher's mind in his moments of speculative excursion. How, for instance, do we consider the objects of sense without some recourse to conceptual activity? This is the challenge the man of commonsense has failed to answer. Hence:

> These empty abstractions of 'singleness' and its antithetic
> 'universality' and also of 'essence', that is attended with
> a 'non-essential' element which is all the same 'necessary',
> are powers the interplay of which constitutes perceptual under-
> standing, often called 'sound commonsense' (*Menschenverstand*)
> which takes itself to be the solid substantial type of con-
> scious life, is, in its process of perception, merely the
> sport of these abstractions; it is always poorest where it
> means to be richest. In that it is tossed about by these
> unreal entities, bandied from one to the other, and by its
> sophistry endeavours to affirm and hold fast alternatively
> now one, then the exact opposite, it sets itself against the
> truth, and imagines philosophy has merely to do with 'things
> of the intellect' (*Gedankendinge*), merely manipulates 'ideas'.
> (PG.MM.105-6/B.176-7)

The appeal to commonsense, far from being the antidote to the abstractions of philosophy, actually involves an even deeper commitment to metaphysical abstractions. Commonsense is no refuge from philosophy; it is only bad philosophy. The main difference between the two camps, says Hegel, is that the philosopher is, at least aware that he is dealing with *Gedankendingen* and is therefore 'master of them'. (PG.MM.106/B.177) (With regard to the dispute between Moore and Bradley, for example, we could say that Bradley was perfectly aware of the time on his watch when he denied the reality of time. Unlike Moore he knew that he was doing philosophy.) But the commonsense realist, says Hegel, 'takes them for the real truth, and is led by them from one mistake to another'. (PG.MM.106/B.177) In this way Hegel draws attention to the language employed by those philosophers who appeal to commonsense in order to debunk metaphysics. For in the texts of those who assert the primacy of commonsense one finds a surprising dependence upon philosophical terminology.[18]

Referring to the abstract language of *commonsense*, Hegel asks us to consider what experience is being described by the expressions 'universality and singleness', and what is this 'essentiality' which is necessarily connected with 'inessentiality'? For in this jargon, says Hegel, lurks a tendency to deceive us about the very nature of experience.

> When understanding tries to give them truth by at one time
> taking their untruth upon itself, while at another it calls
> their deceptiveness a mere appearance due to the uncertainty
> and unreliability of things, and separates the essential from

an element which is necessary to them, and yet is to be inessential, holding the former to their truth against the latter:
when understanding takes this line, it does not secure them
their truth, but convicts itself of untruth. (PG.MM.107/B.178)

Because there is more to the activity of perception than the exercise
the senses, the appeal to *Sinnliche Gegenstanden* belongs to the same
ghostly realm as their allegedly antithetical *Gedankendingen*.

6.   REASON AND OBSERVATION IN HEGEL'S *PHENOMENOLOGY*

If I make an experiment I do not doubt the existence of the
apparatus before my eyes. I have plenty of doubts, but not
that. [Wittgenstein, OC.337]

Perception ends with the recognition that the truth, which has been he
to lie in the thing and its properties, lies elsewhere. In the following section entitled 'Force and Understanding', Hegel considers the
view that the truth rests in force and the play of forces.[19] Percepti
is atomistic; its failure to account for the unity of the thing with i
properties suggests a realm of hidden forces which somehow perform the
task of uniting these properties. As in modern physics the ultimate
reality of a thing is held to be a play of forces. But this reduction
ism is unhelpful since a force cannot be described without some reference to its expression. A knowledge of the forces which lie behind
their manifest expressions presupposes some knowledge of the thing whi
plays host to its forces. We are therefore trapped within the same lo
gical circle of sense-certainty; we have to recognise the thing before
we can describe the forces which are invoked to explain perception.

An explanation of these forces is attempted from the standpoint of
'Understanding', the subsequent stage in the *Phenomenology*. Understan
ding goes beyond exteriority and seeks to discover laws governing the
forces. But again the logical circle returns to plague the realist, f
whilst the object of interest is now an inverted world of forces and
laws, it is necessary to point out that these laws are not distinct fr
the instances falling under them. A knowledge of the supersensible
world of forces and laws cannot serve in any foundational sense since
one cannot isolate the pure law from its instances. Models may be im-
perfect expressions of the law but they are necessary in the sense tha
one needs them to initiate any discussion about the pure law. In
Hegel's hands the world of laws transpires to be a duplication of the
respective world of properties and forces, which is depicted in a bizarre example of an inverted world of supersensible forces and laws.
need not dwell in this world for it is clear that Hegel is driving the
realist perspective to the ultimate in absurdity. The scene is now se

68

for a full-scale attack on the Platonic-Newtonian concept of a universe governed by an unchanging realm of law. The formulation of laws takes place within organised systems of science, not in the private experience of an individual consciousness. It follows that, after methodological solipsism has run its course, the standpoint of *Consciousness* will be transcended by *Self-Consciousness* and later by *Reason*, the standpoint of organised systems of knowledge. Within the standpoint of *Reason*, the perceiving consciousness will be transcended by an observing consciousness, the standpoint of empiricism reflected in the sciences. However, as the *Phenomenology* develops it soon becomes apparent that many of the assumptions of sense-certainty and perception have been carried into the sciences in the guise of an attempt to derive the foundations of science from alleged regularities in nature.

Clearly a detailed analysis of the various shapes of observing consciousness - which takes up over ninety pages of the *Phenomenology* - lie outside the scope of our present inquiry. It would require a familiarity with eighteenth-century science and its philosophical expression in the writings of Hegel's contemporaries and predecessors. Many of the issues that Hegel touches upon are, however, not without contemporary relevance. The status of observational language is examined in physics, biology and psychology. Hegel's treatment of observational language in the physical sciences matches his dialogue with the perceiving consciousness. The experience subjected to phenomenological investigation is not the passive reception of the object; instead the object observed must conform with rational criteria. In genetic terms the consciousness presented within the category of *Reason* is not that of the perceiving infant learning to recognise phenomena, but that of an observer-scientist classifying phenomena and allegedly discovering laws which determine its behaviour. Given this important difference the assumption of immediacy still remains. The rational order of the world is held to stand in an immediate relationship to the rational observer.

The dialectic with the observing consciousness opens with Hegel requesting an explanation of what is considered to be essential or inessential when classifying things. One is reminded of the dialectic with the perceiving consciousness, where Hegel demonstrated how the Perceiver failed to give adequate reasons for drawing his distinction between essential and inessential properties. There, as we have seen, Hegel argued that knowledge of an object's essential properties is not determined by an act of perception, but is a necessary condition of there being any knowledge of the object at all. Confusing essential properties with inessential properties, treating both as sensuously given, the Perceiver failed to demonstrate how one object could be distinguished from another. In the dialectic of observation Hegel subjects the observing consciousness to similar difficulties, asking him to explain how nature reveals those essential characteristics which are considered necessary for the classification of natural phenomena. Classification necessarily precedes scientific explanation. The observer-scientist must start at the beginning. But how can one explain what is considered to be essential or inessential when making the primary classification? Without a principle of selection, the mere act of observation is a pointless exercise. Yet such a principle is not determined by an act of observation. Against the popular belief that scientific practice proceeds from observations to generalisations and laws based upon them, Hegel points out that the scientist actually brings a whole system of rules and a set of sophisticated concepts to bear on his initial observation. Hegel's point is that the laws invoked to explain observed regularities are not determined by the objects observed but from the kind of regularity that exists in human affairs. To speak of regularity and uniformity in nature is not to say that nature is rational, or that an analogy exists between the structure of the world and the comprehending mind. Rationality is determined by human practices: it is a fact about human beings that they could not survive in a world unless they presupposed that it conforms to certain patterns of regularity. The activity of science necessitates rationality in nature. No scientist could admit that nature is beyond the scope of scientific understanding. Irregularities are either ignored or explanations found for them.

When Hegel discusses the truth of the proposition that 'unsuspended objects will fall to the ground' (PG.MM.193/B.290), he makes it clear that this truth is unaffected by observational evidence to the contrary. His argument is similar to Wittgenstein's remarks in *On Certainty* where it is argued that what counts as a truth, such as 'unsuspended objects fall', is not determined by observational criteria. We do not arrive at such truths by repeated observations of falling objects. And if we did observe an occasional stone fly up in the air we would not, says Wittgenstein, suspend our belief that things normally fall to the ground if left unsuspended. As Wittgenstein says:

> even if an irregularity in natural events did suddenly occur,
> that wouldn't *have* to throw me out of the saddle. (OC.619)

That apples fall from trees, stones fall to earth, and water runs downhill, is beyond the range of scientific controversy. Hegel's point is that it makes as little sense confirming it as refuting it. If such facts had to be established, science could never get off the ground, since the possibility of scientific investigation depends upon such assumptions being taken for granted. They form, as Wittgenstein says, the 'scaffolding of our thoughts'. When we throw a stone into a river, or warn someone that a ladder is about to fall, we are excluding the possibility of there being any breakdown in the law of gravity. What counts as a law of nature, providing us with the expectation that it will persist, is not decided after hearing the evidence for or against

it. We do not infer our belief in the uniformity of nature after
listing a number of recorded observations; it is a fundamental feature
of our experience. This is Hegel's position and is what Wittgenstein
had in mind when he referred to the expectation that fire will burn:

> The character of the belief in the uniformity of nature can
> perhaps be seen more clearly in the case in which we fear what
> we expect. Nothing could induce me to put my hand in the
> flame - although after all it is *only in the past* that I have
> burnt myself. (PI.472)
> The belief that fire will burn me is of the same kind as the
> fear that it will burn me. (PI.473)

The uniformity of nature is not justified by observations; it has its
necessity in the fact that if such beliefs were suspended, and if
everything that hung upon them were abstracted away, nothing would remain. There would be no language, no manufacturing processes, nothing
that could be recognised as human activity, and certainly no activity
in which one could speak of deriving the laws of nature from repeated
observations of regularities in the world.

A similar position is developed in Hegel's treatment of biology and
observational psychology. In the former the search for observed regularities turns out to be an unsatisfactory method of classifying organic phenomena, whilst Hegel's examination of observational psychology,
as A. MacIntyre has shown, raises serious doubts about the status of
behaviourist psychology.[20] The conclusion to be drawn is that observational procedures alone cannot reveal the existence of reason in the
world, but that the rationality of nature is to be discovered by looking at the presuppositions built into scientific practice. In this
way the pattern established in the opening chapters of the *Phenomenology*
is repeated. The search for an objective and foundational standpoint
is combatted at each stage with the assertion of the primacy of human
praxis. Eventually the standpoint of *Reason* is transcended by *Spirit*.
It is here that philosophy, presented as absolute knowledge, is considered in its own right. In the following chapter we shall examine
Hegel's conception of philosophy, beginning with his lucid account of
its nature in the *Lectures on the History of Philosophy*.

NOTES

[1] N. R. Hanson, *Patterns of Discovery* (Cambridge University Press,
    1961) p.19.

[2] B. Russell, *Problems of Philosophy,* pp.2-3.

[3] Quoted in *The Lithographer,* July 1965 pp.186-7.

[4] See *Patterns of Discovery*, also 'Causal Chains' by N. R. Hanson in *Mind* 1961.

[5] The following example is a variant of the one provided by Hanson in 'Causal Chains'.

[6] P. K. Feyerabend, 'Problems of Empiricism II', in *The Nature and Function of Scientific Theories, Essays in Contemporary Philosophy* ed. R. G. Colodny, Pittsburg, 1970. pp.284.

[7] Ibid. p.289.

[8] There is a tendency to say that this argument veers towards relativism in the sense that *any* set of beliefs could have a claim to truth. A reflection on the way in which concepts form a system should dispel this view. Consider, for example, the plausibility of the claim that the earth is flat. Suppose the exponent of the flat earth thesis rejects all accounts of sailing around the world as fictitious. His difficulties begin to multiply once we consider the seriousness of his opponents who proceed to build canals at Suez and Panama, organize shipping lines on the principl of a round earth, send satellites into orbit, and so on. When serious men commit themselves to these activities it no longer makes sense to say they are acting on the hypothesis that the earth is round and it makes even less sense to speak of the round earth versus flat earth argument as a disagreement between two equally plausible theories. Human practice reveals that one of them is clearly out of step. If the flat earth thesis were to have a grain of truth so many other institutions would have no reality. In a world of satellites and supersonic flight there is no credibility to the flat earth argument.

[9] *Patterns of Discovery,* p.10.

[10] P. T. Geach, *Mental Acts,* London: Routledge, 1957. p.25.

[11] T. S. Kuhn, *The Structure of Scientific Revolutions,* University of Chicago, 1971. p.113.

[12] This anticipates the following section of the *Phenomenology,* 'Force and Understanding' a standpoint which actually follows from critical realism, but, quite rightly, Hegel defers discussion of it until he has exhausted the possibilities within the standpoint of Perception. To speak of a noumenal world of things as they really are, is a way out of the Perceiver's dilemma, but this would involve a different shape of consciousness than *Wahrnemung.*

[13] Commenting on Wittgenstein's 'the echo of a thought in sight', P. F. Strawson is close to Hegel's position when he says: 'the visual experience is *irradiated* by, or infused with, the concept; or it becomes *soaked* with the concept'. *Freedom and Resentment and Other Essays,* London: Methuen, 1974. p.57.

[14] John Wyndham in 'From Pillar to Post', *Seeds of Time,* Middlesex: Penguin, 1959. p.148.

[15] *The Structure of Scientific Revolutions,* p.85.

[16] Ibid. p.115.

[17] Ibid. p.118.

[18] Similarly one might consider how far removed from ordinary language is the philosophy of ordinary language.

[19] A detailed discussion of the chapter on 'Force and Understanding' lies outside the scope of this inquiry. For a more adequate treatment see D. Murray, 'Hegel: Force and Understanding' in *Royal Institute of Philosophy Lectures,* Vol. 5, 1970-71; H. G. Gadamer 'Hegel's Inverted World', trans. John F. Donovan in *The Review of Metaphysics,* 1975.

[20] See A. MacIntyre, 'Hegel on Faces and Skulls', in *Hegel,* ed. MacIntyre, New York: Doubleday Anchor, 1972.

IV Hegel's conception of philosophy

> The philosopher is a man who must cure himself of many sick-
> nesses of the understanding before he can arrive at the notions
> of the sound human understanding. [Wittgenstein RFM.IV.53]

The best introduction to philosophy, says Hegel, is the study of its
history. This immediately marks philosophy off from many of the empi-
rically-based sciences. A twentieth-century medical student, for example, might be ill-advised to study the methods of his seventeenth-cen-
tury predecessors. At best such a study would be of historic interest
only. For Hegel, however, philosophy possesses an overall unity which
makes it possible to enter the subject at any point in its history. One
can be introduced to philosophical problems concerning human freedom,
knowledge, the good life, and so on by reading Plato or the writings of
contemporary philosophers. One can learn something about the philosophy
of mind from the writings of Kant but a textbook of eighteenth-century
cures for insanity would serve no purposes today and tell us nothing
about the workings of the human mind. Because of the importance Hegel
placed upon an historical presentation this investigation will begin
with his Introduction to the *Lectures on the History of Philosophy*,
looking at his conception of the historical unity of philosophy and its
parallels with several contemporary accounts of philosophical discourse.
In the second section we shall consider Hegel's concept of the 'completion of knowledge', which he postulates as an ideal for the resolution
of philosophical problems. Such a state is only reached after a survey
of the history of philosophy and is described by Hegel as absolute knowledge - a concept which will be examined in the third section of this
chapter. The fourth and fifth sections investigate problems arising
out of Hegel's descriptive approach, with particular reference to the
Phenomenology, where he presented his concept of absolute knowledge by
arranging the various stages of the history of philosophy in an organised system.

In his famous metaphor characterising the development of the Idea,
Hegel depicts the history of philosophy as a

> succession of processes in development which must be represen-
> ted not as a straight line drawn into vague infinity, but a
> circle returning within itself, which, as periphery, has many
> circles whose entire composition consists of a large number
> of processes in development turning back within themselves.
> (GP.I.MM.46/H.27)

In the *Logic* he applies the same metaphor when referring to the development of absolute knowledge.

> By reason of the nature of the method which has been demonstrated the science is seen to be a circle which returns upon itself, for mediation bends back its end into the beginning of simple ground. Further, this circle is a circle of circles, for each member, being simply inspired by the method, is intro-reflection which, returning to the beginning, is at the same time the beginning of a new member. The various sciences, of which each has a before and an after, are figments of a chain, or rather, each *has* only a before, and in conclusion shows its after. (L.MM.571/J&S.484)

According to Hegel the history of philosophy can be represented as a series of circles, or shapes of consciousness, each one reflecting the level of culture and scientific development in its epoch and each one arising out of the previous circle. In this way the history of philosophy can be seen as a series of links in a chain which, in turn, forms a larger circle - the absolute Idea. It is therefore possible to enter philosophy through any of the circles or shapes of consciousness. The metaphor of a circle characterises Hegel's conception of the development of knowledge and philosophy. Just as there are no external foundations to language or systems of scientific knowledge, there are no external foundations of philosophical knowledge. A circle has no beginning and no end. The metaphor suggests that, unlike the empiricist approach, which is represented as a 'straight line drawn into infinity', the Hegelian method does not see philosophy in terms of a progressive accumulation of knowledge.

One of the legacies of pre-Hegelian philosophy is the belief that the sciences, including ethical systems, begin with some theory-neutral or objective foundation upon which further developments are based, and that philosophy is concerned with an investigation into these foundations. The metaphor of a circle calls this assumption into question. If there are no external foundations there can be no external standpoint for the evaluation of statements expressed within a 'circle' of knowledge. Philosophy must be descriptive. A philosopher cannot appeal to any standard external to his shape of consciousness. Operating with this concept of truth, Hegel depicts each stage in the history of philosophy as a complete circle, or shape of consciousness, having its own criterion for the determination of the absolute. Whilst being a reflection of the level of human knowledge and culture relative to its epoch, each shape of consciousness possesses its own standard of knowledge and is not refuted by other stages, although it can be replaced by another shape of consciousness. For Hegel a change in conceptual framework therefore serves as a better description of the development of knowledge than a more perfect interpretation of existing data. In this respect there is a similarity between Hegel's account of developments in philosophy and T. S. Kuhn's account of paradigm switches in scientific revolutions.[1] The philosopher's concern with paradigms or shapes of consciousness is, however, different from the work of a scientist who works within a paradigm. Solving a problem is part of normal scientific activity and a scientist who solves a problem may well return to his former standpoint. On the other hand a philosophica investigation should render it impossible to return to one's former standpoint.[2]

The ultimate reconciliation of the various shapes of consciousness in the Idea finds no parallel with Kuhn's concept of paradigms. Kuhn tend to ignore the relationship between the various paradigms whilst Hegel has his eye on their interrelationships as well as their logical distinctions. There is nothing, however, in Hegel's concept of the Idea which would provide him with serious objections to the following remark by Kuhn and Wittgenstein respectively:

> It cannot be made logically or even probabilistically compelling for those who refuse to step into the circle. The premises and values shared by the two parties to a debate over paradigms are not sufficiently extensive for that. As in political revolutions, so in paradigm choice - there is no standard higher than the assent of the relevant community. To discover how scientific revolutions are attained, we shall therefore have to examine not only the impact of nature and of logic, but also the techniques of persuasive argumentation effective within the quite special groups that constitute the community of scientists.[3]

> When two principles really do meet which cannot be reconciled with one another then each man declares the other a fool and a heretic. (OC.611).

The same sentiment with regard to conflicting philosophical systems is expressed by Hegel when he emphasises the historical relativity of philosophical truth. The difference being that Hegel emphasises the continuity of philosophy and its ultimate reconciliation as well as its sharp conceptual switches.

> ...every philosophy belongs to its own time and is restricted by its own limitations just because it is the manifestation of a particular stage in development...Every philosophy is the philosophy of its own day, a link in the whole chain of spiritual development, and thus it can only find satisfaction for the interests belonging to its own particular time. (GP.I.MM.65/H.45)

One possible objection to Hegel's approach is to denounce it as relativistic. To meet this objection Hegel considers the following questions from a sceptic: 'If every shape in history claims to express the
truth, which one is correct? How can we be certain that any of them
are correct? If we are prohibited from seeking an appeal to a transcendental standard, is not one man's opinion just as good as another
man's?' These are popular objections which find expression in the belief that because philosophy does not appear to make progress like the
empirical sciences, it must be in some sense, subjective and limited
to the expression of opinion. In reply to these objections, Hegel
tells us that 'Philosophy possesses no opinions, for there is no such
thing as philosophical opinions...Philosophy is the objective science
of the truth, the science of necessity'. (GP.I.MM.30/H.12) It is clear
that the reference to an 'objective science of truth' cannot, on
Hegel's terms, refer to the existence of an external court of appeal.
Then how is objective truth to be determined? How is the sceptic to be
answered? Hegel's procedure consists of an attempt to prove the objectivity of philosophical truth asserted within a shape of consciousness by refuting the claim that relativism involves scepticism and subjectivity.

The sceptic's charge can be stated as follows: since every philosophical system has claimed to express the truth, only to be replaced by
another making similar claims, how is it possible to know whether the
truth has been arrived at? And if the great minds have constantly contradicted each other on what basis can *ego homuncio* attempt to form a
judgment? (GP.I.MM.35/H.16) Implicit here, says Hegel, is the rationa-
lization of laziness, since the neglect of study is justified in the
alleged impossibility of arriving at the truth. Also implicit in this
form of scepticism is the view that 'the efforts of philosophy are
futile'. (GP.I.MM.35/H.16) This attitude, says Hegel, is unsuitable
for philosophical inquiry since it rests on a 'superficial view taken
of its history' - a view which is concerned only with the conclusions
drawn after a philosophical investigation not with the investigation
itself. But if we see the history of philosophy as a competition for
the truth then:

> The whole history of philosophy becomes a battlefield covered
> with the bones of the dead; it is a kingdom not merely formed
> of dead and lifeless individuals, but of refuted and spiritually
> dead systems, since each has killed and buried the other.
> (GP.I.MM.35/H.17)

On these grounds the latest philosophical system, being more comprehensive, and having the advantage of reflecting upon the most recent
developments in the sciences, would be the true one. But in this case
its truth would only be momentary.

It often happens that a new philosophy appears on the scene.
This then asserts that the others are not worth considering.
Every philosophy appears not only with the pretension that
through it all previous philosophies are refuted but that their
shortcomings are corrected and that the right one is at last
found. But following upon what has gone before it seems that
other words from the Scripture are equally applicable to the
new philosophy - the words that the Apostle Paul spoke to
Ananias, 'Behold the feet of them that shall carry thee out
are at the door'. Behold the philosophy by which your own will
be refuted and displaced will not wait very long, just as it
has never waited long before. (GP.I.MM.35-6/H.17)

Novelty cannot be accepted as a criterion of philosophical truth.
Hegel's point is this: to see philosophy as a competition for the
truth is to guarantee that one shall never find it. The standards internal to philosophy, like the human history it reflects, cannot be
arrested.

So far it would seem that when faced with different but self-suffi-
cient systems, there can be no criterion for deciding what is true.
But does Hegel's approach have to collapse into scepticism? If this
were the case, argues Hegel, it would strike at the very heart of philosophy. 'The truth', says Hegel, 'is one' and this belief or intui-
tion is correctly held by those who profess scepticism with regard to
the history of philosophy. Unfortunately it is taken to mean that
there is but one truth amidst a variety of incorrect systems, or worse
that there might not be a correct system and philosophy is a waste of
time. In reply Hegel argues that it is a mistake to see philosophy as
the pursuit of the correct answer, that in philosophy the area of interest is both the method as well as the end result. There is here an
analogy between the unity of the search for philosophical truth and
the unity which, according to Kierkegaard - a philosopher often regarded as the antithesis of Hegel - characterises the search for the good.
'If it is possible that a man can will one thing, then he must will
the good', says Kierkegaard.[4] But this does not mean that the good is
one thing to be selected from a number of rival options, and pursued
with relentless exclusion to all else. By expressing the good as one,
Kierkegaard emphasises an internal relation between the means and ends
of ethical conduct in the same way that Hegel emphasises the unity of
a philosophical investigation with the result. Assessing a philosophical truth is like giving an assessment of a person's life. There
is not one standard for the assessment of a life and there is not one
standard for philosophical assessment. Yet this does not rule out the
possibility of making an assessment. It simply means that there are
no hard and fast rules that one can appeal to. The rule book of philosophy will never be published, just as the rule book of ethical

conduct will never achieve universal assent. In a very important sense philosophy is an expression of human life: to speak of a philosophy is to speak of a form of life at a particular stage of its development. Insofar as we can speak of the unity of human life so we can speak of the unity of philosophical expressions of life. When Hegel speaks of the unity of philosophical truth he is asserting the existence of a necessary relationship between philosophical problems which arise at a certain stage of life and the means by which one attempts to find a solution for them.

In opposition to the view that philosophy is a competition for the correct system, Hegel refers to the fact that whilst there are diverse philosophical systems the activity of philosophy exhibits an overall unity. 'Thus whoever may have studied or become acquainted with a philosophy of whatever kind, provided that it is such, has become acquainted with philosophy'. (GP.I.MM.37/H.18) Hegel's point is as simple as it is difficult: despite conceptual transformation the activity of philosophy exhibits an overall unity in aspiration. What appears as a conflict of standards from one standpoint turns out to exhibit a continuity from another standpoint. Revolutions, when viewed from a distance in time, do not exhibit such a rupture with the past as they did to their participants. What appears as an abrupt break with previous philosophical systems often turns out to be very closely related to what has preceded it. In the language of Hegel's *Phenomenology* we might say that *for itself* a philosophical system destroys all that has gone before it, but *for us* - Hegel's readers who are invited to study the history of philosophy in its completeness - there is an unbroken conceptual unity.

Thus Hegel's answer to the charge of subjectivity and scepticism is that the activity of philosophy is that of a continuing conversation. And just like any other conversation what can be said is, to a large extent, governed by what has been said before. Whilst the direction of the conversation may shift there are definite rules governing what can be said next. Not anything can be said and, like any conversation, a shared framework of conventions is presupposed. Meaningful discourse can only take place against a background of shared meanings. Philosophical revolutionaries can overturn the work of their predecessors because there is a shared conception of what would be allowed to count as an overturning of a philosophical tradition. They cannot shake off all conceptual links with the past. Whilst Descartes was widely proclaimed to have broken with his predecessors, there is much in his work which reveals a continuity with his scholastic predecessors. And Wittgenstein's revolution too, is nowadays seen as a development within the idealist tradition rather than a break with the past. It is ironic indeed to note that many Wittgensteinians, whose works are quoted in this text in order to explicate Hegel, would not see themselves in any sense as standing in the same philosophical tradition. And this is Hegel's point: diverse attempts to answer philosophical questions concerning the nature of God, life and morality are all marked by a unity in aspiration unaffected by conceptual reformulation. When the history of philosophy is complete this unity becomes more apparent. The greater the comprehensibility the more the parts of the overall picture fit into place. As Hegel says:

> The stages of the evolution of the Idea, when viewed in a superficial sense, appear to follow each other by accident. This form gives to the stages and development of the Idea the appearance of a haphazard succession of a variety of principles and their execution in their philosophies. But this is not so. For thousands of years this work has been directed by the same architect: and that architect is none other than the living Spirit (*Geist*) whose nature it is to think, and to bring to consciousness what it is and thereby become its object, and at the same time transcending it in itself to a higher stage of its own being. The different systems which the history of philosophy presents are therefore not irreconciliable with unity; they arise partly out of different stages of the development of *one* philosophy at different levels of maturity and partly from the particular principle on which a system is based, but each is a branch of one and the same whole. (Enz.I.13)

Although we can draw logical distinctions between the various shapes o consciousness it is clear from the above remarks that Hegel does not subscribe to the view that each shape is logically autonomous and water-tight - a view which has been wrongly attributed to Wittgenstein account of language games. An analogy between Wittgenstein's concepti of language and Hegel's conception of philosophical discourse can be pursued here. Just as Wittgenstein's language games only have any sen in their interpenetrability with other language games, so Hegel's shap of consciousness exhibit a necessary continuity in the development of history. Hegel's point can be brought out by reference to Renford Bambrough's assertion of:

> ...a physical, historical continuity extending from the primeval slime to Shakespeare and Newton, and with this physical continuity there goes a logical continuity. Since, as a matter of historical fact, there was a gradual development from the primeval slime to Shakespeare, there cannot be a logical gap or discontinuity on the logical scale that connects Shakespeare with the primeval slime.[5]

Bambrough may be overstating his case, especially in the assumption that there is no radical break between the primeval slime and the origins of language, but the point is essentially Hegelian. Bound up with physical and conceptual transformation are many threads of continuity. He makes this point with the example of a resurrected Homer who explains the roughness of the sea with the expression 'Poseidon is angry today'.[6] Over two thousand years later we are capable of understanding this expression, but when we use it, possessed with our knowledge of meteorology and oceanography, we are offering a picturesque description. There is here a logical distinction between the use of the expression as an explanation and its use as a description. In Hegelian terms the modern use of the expression 'Poseidon is angry today' has been mediated by generations of knowledge unavailable to Homer, whilst the former use was mediated by the religious culture appropriate to Homer's epoch. Yet there is a logical continuity in the sense that we can use words like 'anger' for our different purposes. According to Bambrough there are sufficient similarities (family resemblances) between a stormy sea and other cases of anger to justify the use of the term 'anger' in both cases. Like Hegel, Bambrough sees a pattern of continuity stretching across philosophic revolutions and speaks of a close analogy 'between traditional metaphysical philosophy and contemporary epistemological philosophy, and in general for the unity of philosophical enquiry that underlies the plurality and diversity of the idioms in which it has been and is conducted'.[7]

Insofar as the search for philosophical truth exhibits a unity despite a plurality of idioms we can understand why Hegel rejects the sceptical assumption that we may never know which system is the correct one. From the existence of different philosophical systems it does not follow that one alone can or ought to be judged correct, anymore than there can be only one way of living a virtuous life. Hegel likens those who fail to grasp the universal nature of philosophy, and take refuge in scepticism in the absence of any criterion for determining the correct system to

> an invalid recommended by the doctor to eat fruit, and who has cherries, plums, or grapes before him, but who pedantically refuses to take anything because no part of what is offered to him is fruit, some of it being cherries, and the rest plums or grapes. (GP.I.MM.37/H.18)

And in the *Encyclopaedia* he asks:

> Would anyone, who wished for fruit, reject cherries, pears, or grapes, on the ground that they were cherries, pears or grapes, and not fruit? But when philosophy is in question, the excuse of many is that philosophies are so different, and none of them is *the* philosophy - that each is only a

philosophy. Such a plea is assumed to justify any amount of
contempt for philosophy. And yet cherries too are fruit.
(Enz.I.13)

Different philosophical systems are not mutually contradictory. The
philosophy of Plato is not refuted by the philosophy of Wittgenstein
and to see both systems as competitors for the final truth is to miss
the whole point of philosophy. The urge to seek out a criterion for
determining the correct system, says Hegel, arises from holding an 'ab
stract opposition between truth and error', (GP.I.MM.38/H.19) which he
counters in the *Phenomenology* with the following metaphor:

> The bud disappears when the blossom breaks through, and we
> might say that the former is refuted by the latter; in the
> same way when the fruit comes the blossom may be explained
> as a false form of the plant's existence, for the fruit appears
> as its true nature in place of the blossom. These stages are
> not merely differentiated; they supplant one another as being
> incompatible with one another. But the ceaseless activity of
> their own inherent nature makes them at the same time moments
> of an organic unity, where they do not merely contradict one
> another, but where one is as necessary as the other...
> (PG.MM.12/B.68)

So it is with philosophical systems. This is bound up with Hegel's
remark that 'Philosophy can only arise in connection with previous phi
losophy, from which of necessity it has arisen'. (GP.I.MM.22/H.2-3)
Each system is internally related to others by virtue of the universality of philosophy, which is analogous to an organic whole. To grasp
this organic conception of philosophy it is necessary to undertake the
study of the history of philosophy where one discovers that 'competing
systems are actually complementary. If they were not then human history would be an irrational collection of events:

> The facts within history are not adventures and contain no
> more romance than does the history of the world. They are not
> a mere collection of chance events, of expeditions of wandering
> knights, each going about struggling purposelessly, leaving
> no results to show for all their efforts. Nor is it one thing
> that has been thought here, another there at will; and what
> takes place is rational. (GP.I.MM.38/H.19)

Just as the bud is not an isolated event, but an essential feature o
the development of the plant, so is a philosophical system an essentia
feature of the development of spirit. And just as one who has observe
the stages of a plant's development does not see the blossom as a contradiction of the bud, one who has conducted an examination of the

82

various shapes of concsiousness will not see one philosophical system as a contradiction of another, but as incomplete moments in the development of the whole. From *within* each standpoint the truth is absolute, but *for us*, with access to the completed picture, it is incomplete and one-sided. In this way Hegel can be said to tie the solution of philosophical problems to the completion of human knowledge. In the following section we shall consider some of the problems arising out of Hegel's dazzling claim to have achieved this standpoint.

2. THE COMPLETION OF HUMAN KNOWLEDGE

> When philosophy paints its grey in grey, then has a shape of
> life grown old. By philosophy's grey in grey it cannot be
> rejuvenated but only understood. The owl of Minerva spreads
> its wings only with the coming of the dusk. [Hegel, PR. p.10]

What is the nature of Hegel's claim that completed knowledge is attainable and in what sense did he claim to have achieved this standpoint himself? Many commentators have dismissed this as an aberration on Hegel's part. Nevertheless there are two interpretations of Hegel's position. On the one hand there is Kojève's claim that Hegel summed up the history of human thought once and for all - and therefore solved every philosophical problem. On the other hand there is the more moderate view that Hegel claimed to have summed up the history of human knowledge from his own standpoint.

The view that he had attained absolutely complete knowledge is presented by Kojève, who says:

> By understanding himself through the understanding of the
> *totality* of the anthropogenetic historical process, which
> ends with Napoleon and his contemporaries, and by under-
> standing this process through his understanding of *himself*,
> Hegel caused the completed whole of the universal real pro-
> cess to penetrate into his individual consciousness, and then
> he penetrated this consciousness. Thus this consciousness
> became just as total, as universal, as the process that is
> revealed by understanding itself; and this fully self-conscious
> consciousness *is* absolute Knowledge, which, by being developed
> in discourse, will form the content of absolute *philosophy*
> or Science, of that *Encyclopaedia of the Philosophical Sciences*
> that contains the sum of all possible knowledge. [8]

It is, of course, true that Hegel intended the *Phenomenology* as an introduction to 'Systematic Science' by means of an account of the anthropogenetic historical process, but it is doubtful whether he thought, as

Kojève does, of the 'sum of all possible knowledge'. Kojève's position rests on a misunderstanding, or a restricted idea, of Hegel's concept of completed knowledge. For Hegel completed knowledge is infinite, which means that, like a circle, it is without an external limit. It is not to be conceived of as the goal at the end of a straight line, which is the picture Kojève seems to be operating with. Kojève is thinking in terms of a linear progression wherein the completion of human knowledge is a fixed point, the termination of a finite period. Hegel's expression of completed knowledge is not the end of the line, the total sum, but an attempt to show how the various systems of know-ledge form an organic whole. Nowhere did Hegel conceive of a finite limit to human knowledge. His tirades against the attempt to impose limits on human knowledge bear witness to this. The more moderate claim has been advanced by M. Clark, who argues that:

> No interpretation can simply deny that Hegel claimed for the philosopher a final *'Bei-sich-sein'*, a radical unity of the form and content of thought, of philosophy and experience. It was his affirmation of a true interiority, or absolute, even in the most casual of human experience. To mediate the ab-solute one must begin 'absolutely'.
> To conclude this, however, is not necessarily to allow that Hegel's system must represent an unequivocal account of all reality from the point of view at which it is perfectly achieved. Dogmatism of this sort is certainly to be found. But it is far from an adequate account of Hegel's meaning, complex and ambiguous as it was even at the end.[9]

So what did Hegel mean when he claimed to have achieved a completed expression of knowledge? Adopting the moderate thesis Clark relates this claim to Hegel's own standpoint in history.

> How finally, may the interpreter set himself in sympathy before Hegel's apparent claim to put an 'end' to the history of thought with his system? Much must be left to the in-dulgence freely allowed for the exaggerations of all inno-vators, particularly in their polemics. Yet the history of thought is no mere catalogue of succeeding ideas. There re-mains a sense in which thought can take its place in that history only by assuming an absoluteness which sets an 'end' to it. If Hegel held that the limits must be revealed from within, then that may be supposed to have been his attitude to his own historical situation.[10]

But by what right does Hegel claim to have adequately expressed his own historic situation? How do we know that Hegel has 'revealed the limits from within'? If one sees this as a claim to have summed up the entirity of human knowledge from one's own standpoint it would betray an assumption that Hegel was engaged in an encyclopaedic task of adding together the finite range of human knowledge at a specific time. It avoids the difficulty of having to account for future developments in knowledge, which Kojève faces, but it is still unsatisfactory since there is always the possibility of discovering unlimited omissions even from one's own standpoint.

Hegel's claim to have attained complete knowledge does not mean, as Kojève argues, 'that history is completed, that nothing really new can happen in the world'.11 Clark's thesis has the dubious merit of being more modest than Kojève's but as it stands it is inadequate. His argument becomes clear, however, if we consider it in relation to the Preface to the *Philosophy of Right* where Hegel argues that philosophy: 'As the thought of the world...appears only when actuality is already cut and dried after its process of formation has been completed'. (PR. MM.28/K.12-13) Accordingly philosophy, like the owl of Minerva, always arrives when knowledge is complete, since it is only when there is a viable system of knowledge, complete with rules and traditions, that one can philosophise about it. This does not mean that philosophers merely wait on the sidelines until a system of knowledge has come to a definite end. Whilst human knowledge is dynamic and subject to constant change there is a sense in which it is complete at any one of its stages. For this reason philosophy, as the comprehension of completed knowledge, is ever present.

One of the difficulties in grasping Hegel's assertion of completed knowledge stems from a failure to appreciate the nature of the organismic standpoint which Hegel has accepted as the alternative to the atomistic approach. On Hegel's terms talk of completed knowledge, his talk of philosophy appearing when 'actuality is already cut and dried', is not a reference to the end of a finite series. It refers neither to the totality of human knowledge *per se* nor to the totality of knowledge from Hegel's standpoint, of which one can never reach the final sum. The problem here concerns the relationship between the whole and its parts. How can one have knowledge of the whole without knowledge of all of its component parts? Hegel rejects this question. When he speaks of wholes and systems he is not talking about a summation of individual items of knowledge, of aggregates or parts. In summations the parts are recognised by their distinctive qualities but in an organised whole, or system, the parts are connected by means of their position in the system. In aggregates the parts are added; in a system the parts are arranged. The term 'parts' has a different meaning when applied to organised wholes or systems than it does when applied to summations or aggregates. In the former case the term 'parts' can easily be replaced with 'members'; in the latter it cannot. Aggregates and wholes are categorically distinct; the former implies adding, the latter arranging. A concerto is not an aggregate of notes, but an arranged whole.

Grasping, or comprehending, the whole is not the same thing as trying to comprehend an infinite number of parts. One cannot comprehend every single sound in a concerto, but comprehending the concerto as a whole - as distinct from a summation of sounds which include the tapping of the conductor's baton and the applause at the end - is an everyday occurrence.

In every aspect of human experience we encounter wholes that are not necessarily explicable in terms of their component parts. Hegel's point is that human knowledge is characterised not so much by what is experienced but how the latter is arranged. Philosophy as the comprehension of completed knowledge is bound up with the arrangement rather than the summation of ¡items of knowledge. If we avoid the tendency to see Hegel's drive for completed knowledge in Kojève's finite terms it is not unlike Wittgenstein's programme of 'seeing connexions' and re-arranging what is already known. (PI.109, 122)

Hegel's talk of completed knowledge, of philosophy arriving when knowledge is complete, is best understood with reference to his remark that 'the truth is only realised in the form of system'. (PG.MM.28/B.85) Instead of seeing the completion of human knowledge in terms of an accumulation of particular items of information in an encyclopaedia - the completeness of which can always be disputed - Hegel's point is that we should see it, as we do in every walk of life, as an organised system. Knowledge is only real if it is presented by a mediating subject in the form of a system. This is why Hegel insists that 'Substance is subject' that there is no substance other than that created by a mediating subject, whether it be the subject expressed as self-consciousness or as world spirit. (PG.MM.23/B.80) As Hegel says:

> That the truth is only reached in the form of a system, that substance is essentially subject, is expressed in the idea which represents the absolute as spirit (*Geist*) - the grandest of all conceptions, and one which is due to modern times and its religion. Spirit is the only reality. (PG.MM.28/B.85)

The completion of human knowledge which Hegel sees as the satisfactory solution to philosophical puzzlement is not a final state, akin to the day when the library is full. Like Wittgenstein, Hegel saw the solution to philosophical puzzlement in the rearrangement of the books according to some system or rule. Hegel's assertion of completed knowledge is thus tied to his version of idealism. Reality is rational because its form is a product of human knowledge. The aspiration towards completeness runs counter to any philosophy which asserts the inadequacy of human beings. Thus Hegel's claim that he, and his reader are in possession of completed knowledge is a rejection of theories which postulate the limits of human reason.

The proof of Hegel's claim lies in the presentation of the sequence of shapes of consciousness in the *Phenomenology* where he attempts to show how they develop out of each other according to 'reason's purposive activity'. (PG.MM.26/B.83) The *Phenomenology* can thus be read as the intellectual history of mankind wherein, as in some epic plot, the particular shapes of consciousness make their appearance and unwittingly set into motion the forces of the shape that will replace them, and subsequently bow out. Since the essence of Hegel's phenomenological method is to 'make no contribution' one might ask whether we are observing nothing more than a 'parade of shapes' where each one becomes aware of its limits and therefore adopts a new standpoint? This interpretation is advanced by I. Soll who says:

> An unsuccessful attempt to give linguistic expression to one of the forms of consciousness in the *Phenomenology* provides the necessary impetus for *progress* to a higher form. For Hegel the limits of language are laudable.[12]

This view, however, presupposes the existence of a standard external to discourse, external to each shape, with which one could assess the adequacy of a shape. It would be equivalent to knowing that language and knowledge were smaller in compass to the world, a view which sounds plausible until we ask 'How does one speak of that which is beyond the scope of language and thought?' Against Soll's interpretation it must be pointed out that for Hegel each shape expresses its content, its language is adequate and is capable of developing a self-critique. It is only from another standpoint that a former shape appears to have been inadequately expressed. At this point the analogy with paradigm changes in science is relevant: Kuhn, for example, points out that many 'of the puzzles of normal science did not exist until after the most recent scientific revolution...Earlier generations pursued their own problems with their own instruments and their own canons of solution'.[13] Soll's account on the other hand makes it appear that each shape fails to capture reality; that it knows itself to be wrong, whereas for Hegel, like Kuhn, the opposite is the case. Each shape determines what is to count as true or false, and is perfectly adequate until another one is adopted. Hegel's reference to 'reason's purpose', to the 'cunning of reason', is never to some future goal externally directed, but to what is brought about by each shape, often breaking up into internal contradictions, but nevertheless acting in accord with its own standards of rationality. Hegel's way of saying this is to say that the absolute is ever present, always realising itself, and that:

> Each of the parts of philosophy is a philosophical whole, a circle rounded and complete in itself. In each of these parts, however, the philosophical Idea is found in a particular specificality or medium. The single circle, because it is a real totality, bursts through the limits imposed by its special

medium, and gives rise to a wider circle. The whole of philosophy in this way resembles a circle of circles. The Idea appears in each circle, but at the same time, the whole Idea is constituted by the system of these particular phases, and each is a necessary member of the organization. (Enz.I.15)

3. THE ABSOLUTE

> We shall not cease from exploration
> and the end of all our exploring
> Will be to arrive where we started
> And to know the place for the first time.
>> [T. S. Eliot, 'Little Gidding',
>> *Four Quartets,* lines 239-43]

A great deal of nonsense has been written about Hegel's absolute Idea. Yet Hegel sees the absolute as nothing more than the method of conducting philosophical inquiry.

> To speak of the absolute Idea may suggest the conception that we are at length reaching the right thing and the sum of the whole matter. It is certainly possible to indulge in a lot of senseless declamation about the Idea absolute. But its true content is only the whole system of which we have been hitherto studying the development (Enz.I.237)

One of the points Hegel is making is that the result of a philosophical investigation is determined by the criteria employed in the investigation; that what is found out in philosophy is internally related to the medium and the method by which it is found out. Just as his absolute spirit is not some external cosmic force, so absolute knowledge is not an Archimedian standpoint external to philosophical discourse. We can bring out what Hegel has in mind here by reference to a paper on Hegel's *Logic*, by A. R. Manser,[14] in which he draws attention to the internal relation between the absolute and the means of reaching it. According to Manser there is a sense in which the absolute 'is not the goal of the search but rather something which belongs internally to the search as such. One could put this by saying that in philosophy it is always internal relations with which we are concerned, never merely external ones. The errors and confusions in philosophy come from thinking of internal relations as external'.[15] The nature of this confusion can be brought out by the following example:

> One way of looking at human life is to think of it as a search for something, an effort to attain some position, status or

whatever and this need is seen as something external to the life activity itself. We might put this in a more popular way by thinking of the following example: I come across a map which shows where some treasure is located. I undertake a great amount of research to discover which island is represented on the map and whether there is a good reason to believe that the pirates buried their treasure in that area. I find that there is some evidence for this so I get an expedition together to visit the island and we dig in the right place and find it. We have the treasure so the search itself is no longer important. We have achieved our aim and so how the search was conducted is of merely historical interest because the finding of the treasure was its end, an end which exists independently of the search. After all the treasure was there all the time whether anyone was looking for it or not and it might have happened that somebody stumbled on the treasure the day before we arrived on the island. Then he would have it and we would not. This would have rendered all our search and research futile. Similarly, if one looks on one's life as the search for a particular definable state then failure to attain this may render the whole of that life meaningless and this is because the goal of the life was seen as something externally related to it. The same thing obviously applies to the concept of reward after life. I take it that this was the internal relationship between ethical reward and the action whether in this life or in another that Wittgenstein was referring to in *Tractatus* 6.422.

"The first thought in setting up an ethical law of the form 'thou shalt...' is: and what if I do not do it. But it is clear that ethics has nothing to do with punishment and reward in the ordinary sense. The question as to the *consequences* of an action must therefore be irrelevant. At least these consequences will not be events. For there must be something right in that formulation of the question. There must be some sort of ethical reward and ethical punishment, but this must lie in the action itself. (And this is clear also that the reward must be something acceptable, and the punishment something unacceptable)."

If one looks on the absolute in philosophy as something external to the activity of philosophising then you have made the same sort of mistake as I have been discussing here. Because the absolute is not something unrelated to the activity of philosophising it is that activity itself.[16]

The above example reveals how Hegel's concept of the absolute-as-method is relevant to the Wittgensteinian period of philosophy. But more

significant is the fact that such examples reveal where it is incorrect
to place emphasis upon the end result, that in many cases the method
employed is of equal, if not greater importance. Now the significance
of Hegel's emphasis upon the method of inquiry is misunderstood by
those who hold that it is the philosopher's task to tell us something
about the structure of an independent reality. They complain that
Hegel shirked his responsibilities when he equated the absolute with
philosophy itself. This is reminiscent of Russell's complaint that the
later Wittgenstein had abandoned the philosophical task of determining
the nature and structure of reality in favour of linguistic inquiries.
In *My Philosophical Development*, Russell tells how he finds Wittgenstein's *Philosophical Investigations* 'completely unintelligible', and
confesses a failure to 'understand why a whole school finds important
wisdom in its pages'.[17] He adds:

> Although I feel strongly about the importance of analysis, this
> is not the most serious of my objections to the new philosophy.
> The most serious of my objections is that the new philosophy
> seems to me to have abandoned, without necessity, that grave and
> important task which philosophy throughout the ages has hitherto
> pursued. Philosophers from Thales onwards have tried to under-
> stand the world. Most of them have been unduly optimistic as
> regards their own successes. But even when they have failed,
> they have supplied material to their successors and an incentive
> to new effort. I cannot feel that the new philosophy is carry-
> ing on this tradition.[18]

According to Russell the later Wittgenstein was only concerned with the
means of understanding the world. From a later standpoint it is apparent that Wittgenstein's inquiries into the nature of language were
simply another way of understanding the world and the gap between the
two philosophies is not as wide as it was felt to be at the time when
Russell complained of Wittgenstein's unintelligibility.

Just as Russell claimed that Wittgenstein's descriptions of linguistic practices had missed the point of philosophical inquiry so have
prominent Hegelians maintained that Hegel's descriptive dialectics has
somehow missed the point of philosophy. Consider McTaggart's objection
to Hegel's account of the absolute-as-philosophical-method.

> Many students must have expressed some disappointment when,
> turning to the end of the *Philosophy of Spirit,* they found
> that its final stage was simply philosophy. It is true that
> any thinker, who has the least sympathy with Hegel, must assign
> to philosophy a sufficiently important place in the nature
> of things. Hegel taught us that the secrets of the universe
> opened themselves to us, but only on condition of deep and
> systematic thought, and the importance of philosophy was un-
> diminished either by scepticism or by appeals to the healthy

instincts of the plain man. But there is some difference between taking philosophy as the supreme and adequate means, and admitting it to the supreme end. There is some difference between holding that philosophy is the knowledge of the highest form of reality, and holding that it is itself the highest form of reality.[19]

McTaggart therefore concludes that:

Hegel has been untrue to the tendencies of his own system in seeking the ultimate reality of Spirit in philosophy alone, and that, on his own premises, he ought to have looked for a more comprehensive explanation.[20]

It is certainly true that prominent Hegelians, at the close of the nineteenth-century, operated with a means-ends distinction, at least in the moral sphere. Consider how the means-ends distinction appears in the moral philosophy of Bradley and McTaggart, who both saw morality in purposive terms. Ironically, when J. L. Stocks criticised their 'purposive' means-ends distinction he was closer to Hegel than his Hegelian adversaries. Speaking of the Bradleyian thesis of moral perfectibility as an end, Stocks said:

that there may well be such an aim, and it may well be considered more important than riches, but it is after all only an end, like any other, a possible result of action, and that it falls, with all other ends, under the inflexible moral rule that it may not be purchased by any and every means. Morality may call on a man at any moment to surrender the most promising avenue to his own moral perfection.[21]

Stocks' point about moral perfection being inseparable from the means is Hegel's point about the absolute being inseparable from the method. The absolute end is not out of reach, a 'beyond' lying outside of our finite categories, nor is it an ultimate and perfect state of being. The absolute is within human grasp if only we are prepared to acknowledge it and abandon the search for a transcendental standpoint - just as moral perfection is to be found in our ways of seeking it, rather than in some distinct end. This is what Hegel means in the following remarks:

The finitude of the end consists in the circumstance, that, in the process of realising it, the material, which employed as the means is only externally subsumed under it and made conformable to it. But as a matter of fact, the object is the concept implicitly: and thus when the concept, in the shape of the end, is realised in the object, we have but the

91

manifestation of the inner nature of the object itself. Objectivity is thus, as it were, only the husk under which the concept lies concealed. Within the range of the finite we can never see or experience that the end has been really secured. The consummation of the infinite end, therefore consists merely in removing the illusion which makes it seem yet unaccomplished. (Enz.I.212)

Like Wittgenstein, Hegel is here suggesting that the absolute, philosophical satisfaction, is achieved by the method which removes the illusions (misleading pictures) which prevent us from seeing it. It is not that there are limits which rule out comprehension, but that these limits are illusory. Moreover, it is not the case that there are limits which, with effort, can be surpassed. This would place absolute knowledge in the sphere of the contingent, and philosophy would remain on a par with the other sciences, a vehicle for the discovery of facts which are inexplicable to them. On the contrary, absolute knowledge, the satisfaction to philosophical problems, is in a very important sense, before us all the time, manifesting itself in the various systems of knowledge. Despite the obscure terminology with which Hegel shrouds his account of the absolute there is, in his account of the standard for achieving philosophical satisfaction, a similarity with Wittgenstein's method of redirecting the philosopher from the starry heavens to lived reality. The ultimate standards of philosophical inquiry turn out to be before us all the time, just as:

The Good, the absolutely Good, is eternally accomplishing itself in the world: and the result is that it need not wait upon us, but is already by implication, as in full actuality accomplished. This is the illusion under which we live. (Enz.I.212)

Like Wittgenstein, Hegel maintained that philosophical satisfaction could be attained by removing illusions and transcendental yearnings in a return to lived reality. To this end Hegel advocated a purely phenomenological method.

4. THE DIFFICULTY WITH HEGEL'S PHENOMENOLOGY

After several unsuccessful attempts to weld my results together into such a whole, I realised that I should never succeed. The best that I could write would never be more than philosophical remarks; my thoughts were soon crippled if I tried to force them on in any single direction against their natural inclination. And this was, of course, connected with the very nature of the investigation. [Wittgenstein, PI.vii]

> True scientific knowledge, on the contrary, demands abandonment
> to the very life of the object, or, which means the same thing,
> claims to have before it the inner necessity controlling the
> object, and to express this only. [Hegel, PG.MM.52/B.112]

Hegel's commitment to a rigorous phenomenology is outlined in the
Introduction to the *Phenomenology* where he promises that the following
presentation of the entire range of shapes of consciousness will 'indicate the nature of absolute knowledge itself'. (PG.MM.81/B.145) It
has been argued that absolute knowledge is not a superior standpoint
but merely an expression of Hegel's method of practising philosophy.
There is, however, a suggestion that Hegel, like Wittgenstein, may have
believed he had put an end to philosophy - insofar as philosophy was
held to be concerned with the search for external and transcendental
standards of certitude. But one of the problems with a purely descriptive method is that the need for further description is without limit.
Despite Wittgenstein's imaginative descriptions of the workings of language not one philosophical problem has been laid to rest. Linguistic
alienation remains, and the tendency to reify thought and the yearning
for transcendental absolutes is forever manifesting itself. This is
one of the reasons why Marx, when criticising the Hegelians, maintained
that the cure for philosophical sickness cannot come from within philosophy but from changes in the social structure. There is evidence that
Wittgenstein too, held that ultimately philosophical alienation could
only be overcome by social or technological change. In the *Remarks on
the Foundations of Mathematics* he says:

> The sickness of a time is cured by an alteration in the mode
> of life of human beings, and it was possible for the sickness
> of philosophical problems to get cured only through a changed
> mode of thought and of life, not through a medicine invented
> by an individual.
>   Suppose the use of the motor-car produces or encourages
> certain illnesses, and mankind is plagued by such illness until,
> from some cause or other, as the result of some development or
> other, it abandons the habit of driving. (RFM.II.4)

It is clear that Wittgenstein, like Marx, recognised that the solution
to philosophical alienation could not be resolved by the efforts of an
individual philosopher. Before completing the *Phenomenology* Hegel
must have become aware of these problems. Like Wittgenstein his method
demanded complete abandonment to the problem in hand. The result was
that in the *Phenomenology* he was obliged to embrace more and more
shapes of consciousness, as philosophical problems multiplied instead
of decreasing. The work, which Müller has compared with 'the eruption
of a volcano',[23] was hurriedly written in the summer of 1806. It grew
out of control. Pressed by his publishing contract Hegel sent an

unbalanced work to the publishers.[24] Several months later he submitte
a Preface which attempted to restore coherence and unity to the work
and to give an account of his conception of philosophy as presented in
the *Phenomenology*.

Walter Kaufmann describes Hegel's idea of organising all viewpoints
in an ascending ladder as an enterprise that is 'as dazzling to contem
plate as it is mad to implement'.[25] Yet notwithstanding the enormity
of the task Hegel only intended it to serve as the introduction to Vol
ume I of *Speculative Philosophy or Logic and Metaphysics*. However, th
book grew out of all proportion to Hegel's original intentions. Kaufmann, who argues that Hegel had lost his way as early as the chapter o
the 'Unhappy Consciousness', says:

> The reader forgets the image of a ladder and wonders which of
> the many features of the tableau are in any sense necessary
> and essential to this stage; and the author too, has plainly
> lost sight of the idea and plan of his work, and far from com-
> prehending his exposition severely dwells at unnecessary
> length on irrelevancies.[26]

Kaufmann's conclusion is that contrary to McTaggart's account of Hege
dialectic as a system of philosophy,[27] Hegel is actually unsystematic

> He assumes that philosophy requires a distinctive method of
> its own and writes as if he had such a method; but in fact,
> as we follow his procedure closely, we find that he did not.[28]

It is questionable whether Hegel did assume that philosophy required a
distinctive method but the content of Kaufmann's main charge is correc
There is too much accidental material in the *Phenomenology* and a lack
of order which reveals the inherent difficulty in providing an orderly
presentation of the sequence of shapes and an inadequate treatment of
the philosophical problems relative to them. In his later letters
Hegel was to criticise the lack of structure and form in the *Phenomeno
logy*,[29] but as late as 1831 when he began preparations for a second
edition he made a note for himself saying, 'Unusual early work, not to
be revised'.[30] It is clear that Hegel wished to retain the *Phenomenology* in its old form but did not see it as the first part of a system.
In fact when he revised for the new edition of the *Phenomenology* in
1831 he stuck out the phrase 'as the first part of the system of
science'. The *Phenomenology* was originally intended as a ladder to th
standpoint of philosophy which, in the course of writing became a majo
work of philosophy capable of existing alongside the *Logic* - his secon
attempt at a system - and his other works. For this reason there were
no major revisions of the *Phenomenology*. The *Logic* is not the second
part of the system, it is the second attempt to produce one.

It is often forgotten that Hegel was an unsystematic thinker domina-
ted more by the material at hand than by the need to produce an overall
system. According to Kaufmann, Hegel found it extremely difficult to
finish any book.

His first attempt, the *Phenomenology of Spirit,* published when
he was thirty-six, was presented as the first part of a system,
of which the second part never appeared; the conception of
the book changed radically while he wrote it; and it still bears
the imprint of his native highly unsystematic bent. In his
second attempt, the *Logic,* he achieved a far greater degree of
order, by the ingenious device of labelling his constant di-
gressions, many of them fascinating essays, 'Notes'. In the
first volume of the *Logic* he interspersed over thirty 'Notes';
and by the time he reached the third and final volume he was
doing something altogether different from what he had done in
the first two. After that he stopped writing books. He published two more volumes, to be sure, - both of them syllabi
marked clearly on the title page 'To be used in connection with
his lectures'. The great bulk of his posthumously published
collected 'works' is due to the inclusion of his lectures,
published by his students, largely on the basis of their own
notes. Finding that he never adhered to the same order twice,
they not only collated notes of different years but felt free
- for example, in the lectures on aesthetics - to impose systematic arrangements of their own.[31]

In a study of the composition of the *Phenomenology* Otto Pöggeler has
drawn attention to several connections between the imbalance of the
chapters in the *Phenomenology* and its status in relation to the *Logic.*[32]
Pöggeler cites Hegel's changing titles for its changing role.[33] And he
also argues that Hegel changed his mind about the role of the *Phenomenology* as he wrote it. Evidence for this, says Pöggeler, can be seen in
the increasing lengths of the chapters.[34] But on the other hand there
is evidence from Hegel's own words that he envisaged the problem of in-
creasingly extending chapters owing to the need to draw together wider
and wider systems. At the end of the chapter on 'Consciousness' Hegel
says:

It will be equally evident that to get acquainted with what
consciousness knows when it is knowing itself, requires us
to fetch a still wider compass. What follows will set this
forth at length. (PG.MM.136/B.213)

Insofar as the *Phenomenology* represents an attempt to redirect natural
consciousness away from the concept of philosophy as a science of objective necessity the optimism of the Introduction expressed in the belief that this could be achieved in the presentation of a series of

shapes, gives way to a doubt that his standpoint of philosophy could never be achieved in an introduction to Systematic Science. The *Phenomenology* was intended to put an end to the craving for transcendental certainty, but by the time he had reached the second half it was beginning to look as if the human mind would never grasp the idea of truth as an organic and systematic whole.

Commenting on the sections concerned with Observing Reason Müller says:

> The major theme in the middle part of Hegel's book is the grim and pessimistic critique of the incompetence of man. In principle ('in itself') comprehension understands reality as a beloved and loving, organic whole, in which all individuating forms of life will be known in their contribution to this 'we that is I'. But alas! in practice, comprehension (*Vernunft*) fails most miserably. It only 'observes' vague analogies to itself in external teleological relations; or in equally vague interpretations of physical appearance, body types, bone structures as clumsy expressions of soul or life.35

The grounds for this pessimism are evident in Hegel's investigation of Observing Reason, where Hegel combats rigid distinctions drawn between theory and observation; between the structures and functions of organic phenomena which were then assumed to provide a natural foundation for the biological sciences; where external teleologies were sought instead of comprehending organic activity in terms of mutually interacting systems. As Müller notes, at every level of the *Phenomenology* one finds Hegel combatting the desire for external truths: the chapter on 'Self-Consciousness' ended with the 'Unhappy Consciousness' seeking a transcendental God; 'Reason' ends with the search for an impersonal moral law; whilst in the cultural, or Spiritual world, the freedom of the Enlightenment leads to terror and attempts to impose a super-standard by means of external force. Finally the shapes of consciousness seek certainty in divine revelation. The entire *Phenomenology*, both at the subjective and social stages of consciousness, epitomises human desire for external absolute standards.

Like Wittgenstein, Hegel had a great respect for the constant striving to express the inexpressible and recognised that the assertion of transcendental certainties would repeat themselves in all aspects of human knowledge. And like Wittgenstein he recognised that the only way to satisfy transcendental cravings is to let these concepts work themselves out. For this reason the Hegel-Wittgenstein 'voyage of discovery' is an unsystematic wandering over the landscape of human thought and language. But unlike Wittgenstein, Hegel's interest in science and history enabled him to recognise the existence of certain similarities between the problems confronting him during the various stages of his wanderings. Whilst his method was purely descriptive - to the point of not being a method - a pattern in his 'voyage of discovery' was truly emerging. The more details he filled in the more unified and complete the picture became. The journey began to have a direction of its own. It was important that something should be said about this emerging pattern: the Preface reveals Hegel's attempt to draw attention to this phenomenon. As Müller observes:

> The Introduction expresses the original intention to describe the experience which human consciousness as soul or subjective mind makes with itself in reaching the comprehensive standpoint of philosophy. The Preface, overlooking the whole production, imparts to it an aesthetic unity which the whole story acquired unintentionally.36

One might suppose that this contradicts Kaufmann, and indeed Hegel's own criticism of the lack of structure in the *Phenomenology*. But the vision acquired on the journey is not marred by the fact that one had occasionally lost the route. The problem is, however, that of presenting this vision without drawing too much attention to those moments when it appeared to be obscure. So in the Preface we find Hegel drawing attention to a unity of history's philosophical strivings which have been clouded over in the main text by Hegel's tendency to write longer on one topic than another. It is, nevertheless, precisely the undirected unity of the work - in spite of the author's tendency to follow the argument wherever it led - which gives an extra meaning to the claim that 'the truth is the whole'. This claim is not only a guiding principle of the method, but a conclusion drawn from a presuppositionless description of the succession of shapes presented in the *Phenomenology*. Breaking his own rule forbidding the prefacing of philosophical theses, Hegel offers a condensed version of his work. But he makes it clear that this condensed version has no force; that nothing can stand as a substitute for the 'inner necessity' of the concept; that the Preface is only for those who have already reached the standpoint arrived at by the author of the book.

We can therefore read the Preface as a last-ditch attempt to prevent Hegel's presentations from congealing into a formal system, and as an attack on the attempt to determine abstractly, the truth or falsity of a philosophical work. Instead, Hegel reminds the reader that one should have no specific method, that philosophy should be purely descriptive, and that the only standards in his book are those employed within the shapes of consciousness he describes. We cannot test the truth of the *Phenomenology* because, like Wittgenstein's *Investigations*, there is no method to test. (One may, however, repudiate this way of doing philosophy but that is another matter). In this way Hegel begins, and ends, the Preface by warning the reader not to expect absolute

knowledge at the end of the work, if by 'absolute knowledge' one means
something that can be defined at the outset of a philosophical investigation. By this time Hegel knew that his contemporaries were waiting
for him to produce the definitive system. The Preface is an eleventh
hour attempt to avoid this kind of misconception. Ironically he knew
that his work would be accepted as one system amongst others; hence
his polemic against the reviewers towards the end of the work.

5. THE UNITY OF METHOD AND CONTENT: THE PREFACE TO HEGEL'S PHENOMENOLOGY

> ...whatever it might be suitable to state about philosophy in
> a preface...cannot be accepted as the form and manner in which
> to expound philosophical truth. (PG.MM.11/B.68)

According to Hegel, knowledge is characterised by the operation of
thought upon its object. This rule applies to all branches of knowledge, including philosophy. The specific relationship between the
knowing subject and the object under investigation distinguishes the
type of knowledge in question. But what is it that marks a distinction
between, for example, morality, aesthetics, religion, and philosophy?
The difference between them, according to the *Phenomenology*, is not one
of kind but the degree of completeness between the subject and the object. Thus in sense-experience the object is furthest away from the
subject, and with absolute knowledge (philosophy), as we have seen,
the subject and object are one and the same. In the empirical sciences
we might say, thought and its object can be related in many ways,
according to the nature of the objects within each particular discipline. Astronomy, for example, is largely determined by the behaviour
of the planets, and its truth agreed upon by reference to the planets.
Taxonomy, however, has a greater degree of arbitrariness, religion and
aesthetics bring the knowing subject into even greater prominence, but
philosophy is the only subject wherein there is nothing externally objective for the truth to be anchored. The object of philosophy is the
absolute, which is to say that philosophy itself is the object of a
philosophical inquiry. It may be true that philosophers have sought an
objective ground for philosophy, but the *Phenomenology* reveals the
difficulties inherent in the foundationalist approach. The outcome is
that philosophy appears to be a loose and freewheeling activity. In
philosophy, argues Hegel, the method and content are one and the same:
in the other sciences it may be possible to distinguish between the
method and content.It is possible, for example, to separate proposition
concerning the planets from the method of observing the planets. The
planets as such are not entirely dependent upon the methods employed by
astronomers who observe them - although many theories concerning plane-
tary motions have a greater degree of arbitrariness than classical
physics once supposed. One can know something of the planets without

acquiring the skills and theories possessed by an astronomer. Moreover, if we define astronomy as the science of the planets and other heavenly bodies we may not have said much about astronomy, but we would have indicated the kind of activity it is. If a child asked 'What kind of an activity is astronomy?' one would convey some information by telling him that astronomers study the heavens. If someone were to ask 'What is philosophy?' and we reply with 'The study of the absolute, the study of reality, or the study of other philosophical systems' we have conveyed no information at all. We cannot say what philosophers do without engaging in philosophy ourselves, without committing oneself to a particular philosophical position. For this reason propositions concerning the object of philosophy, its value and status, cannot be distinguished from the activity of philosophy itself. One of Hegel's reasons for describing philosophy as a circle that turns back on itself is because one can only understand propositions concerning the object of philosophy if one is already within the sphere of philosophy. And then, perhaps, the initial question presupposes that one knows already.

For the above reasons Hegel opens the Preface to the *Phenomenology* with the seemingly paradoxical assertion that one cannot preface a philosophical thesis. The first step inside Hegel's philosophy is the comprehension that there can be no initial step. To take that step implies that one is there already. The reasoning behind this paradox concerns the fact that the object and method are internally related in such a way that there is no way of describing the object without reference to the method. What does this mean? Consider engineering where the goal might be the construction of a bridge. The means by which this goal is reached are inessential from the standpoint of the engineer; they are simply factors which can be weighed up against other factors. But in philosophy the area of interest is precisely those demonstrable proofs by means of which the end may or may not be reached. The means, in philosophy, are the ends; they are the real object of study. A philosopher may claim to be giving an account of reality, the absolute, and so on, but this is really inessential. The area of interest actually centres on the proofs (his arguments), examples, and assumptions employed in the advancement of his thesis. Merely to ask for his conclusions, as one would ask an economist, physician, engineer, and so on, is to miss the whole point of philosophy. The objective, or goal, is expressed in the road upon which one travels towards the destination, but there is no ultimate destination for the road is circular; it is infinite.

In a very important respect Hegel's conception of philosophy as a unity of method and content bears a striking resemblance to some remarks of St. Augustine, quoted by Wittgenstein to express his attitude towards philosophy:

99

...quia plus loquitur inquisitio quam inventio...[38]

It is therefore important to grasp this distinction between philosophy and other disciplines, since much confusion over the nature of Hegel's absolute at the end of the *Phenomenology* stems from precisely this area. Hegel's absolute is the actual method of doing philosophy. Against the charge that one need only be concerned with results in phi losophy, Hegel's reply in the Preface to the *Phenomenology* is that even in the other sciences the results are never entirely distinct fro the means:

> because philosophy is essentially concerned with the universal in which the particular is enclosed, it seems, in the case of philosophy more than the other sciences, that the end or final results give expression to the subject matter itself, even as if they have adequately expressed its very essence, contrasted with that the mere process of working things out may seem to be inessential. Yet on the other hand it is not thought that the general idea of e.g. anatomy - the knowledge of the parts of the body considered in their lifeless existence - automatically provides us with an adequate knowledge of the subject matter itself. On the contrary, if we want possession of the contents of this science, we must, above all, be concerned with the particulars. (PG.MM.11/B.67)

In the absence of any definable subject matter of philosophy we cannot speak of the correct, or incorrect, method of approaching it. To do so would imply an external and indubitable standard, a further meta physical standpoint, to which one could appeal. Moreover, as Hegel points out, when one tries to determine the relationship between one's own philosophical work and another's, an alien element is drawn into the matter. The reader, who intends to judge between two philosophica theses in terms of their respective accuracy in depicting the object their enquiry, mistakenly assumes a rigid distinction between truth ar falsity. This, says Hegel, is because he assumes the existence of an object, or standard external to the system in which it is presented. When confronted with a description of two philosophical accounts of reality he therefore assumes one to be true and the other false. But this is not the case with philosophical systems, or philosophical accounts of reality. Hegel illustrates this with his famous organic metaphor.

> The bud disappears when the blossom breaks through, and we might say that the former is refuted by the latter; likewise, when the fruit comes, the blossom may be explained as a false form of the plant's existence... (PG.MM.12/B.68)

100

ut as Hegel points out, their fluid form reveals that they are not
contradictory but are complementary in the life of the whole. Analo-
ously, philosophical systems are only seen as antithetical or
utually exclusive because of the tendency to view philosophy in terms
f the fixed conceptions which have been taken from other disciplines.
et in philosophy, as Hegel and Wittgenstein would agree, the essential
oncern is not with the truth or falsity of the conclusion of a philo-
ophical investigation. For this reason those who feel inclined to
rgue that Kant was right as opposed to Hume, or that Wittgenstein's
nvestigations is correct as opposed to the *Tractatus*, are missing the
oint of philosophy. In fact this is a frequent occurrence which is
ue to the tendency amongst philosophers towards discipleship. Con-
ider, in this respect, Rush Rhees's criticism of Pitcher's distinction
etween the early and later Wittgenstein. In *The Philosophy of Witt-*
enstein Pitcher implied that the *Tractatus* was wrong whilst the *Inves-*
igations offered a more correct approach. Says Rhees:

> The *Investigations* might have helped him. But he sees
> Wittgenstein here demolishing his earlier system and erec-
> ting a new one. (p.187) Whereas Wittgenstein would have
> demolished, if he could, the idea of philosophical discussion
> as a contest to settle who's right and who's wrong.[39]

f we ignore the paradox involved in saying that Pitcher was wrong, the
oint is essentially Hegelian. It serves no purpose in philosophy to
etermine the correctness of a system solely in terms of the results.
f one were to preface a philosophical system it would involve giving
n explanation of the end without reference to the method. To be con-
erned with results, says Hegel, is to be concerned with the 'corpse of
 system that has left its guiding tendency behind it'. (PG.MM.13/B.69)
 description of the end or purpose is mistaken because 'the real sub-
ect matter is not exhausted in its purpose but in working the matter
ut; nor is the result attained the actual whole itself, but only the
esult together with the process of arriving at it'. (PG.MM.13/B.69)
hat is important for philosophy as well as being its distinctive
haracteristic, is the interest in the steps taken. But the method it-
elf cannot be presented and judged on its correctness, since the cor-
ectness is inseparable from the method.

How is it possible to assess a philosophical system if one can iso-
ate neither the method nor the content? The search for external cri-
eria is rejected by Hegel whose phenomenological approach insists on
he presentation of each philosophy on its own terms. But again the
harge of subjectivism and relativism raises its head. Has not Hegel
bolished all external criteria leaving the standard of correctness
pen to each philosopher's whim and caprice? On the other hand Hegel
as something critical to say about every philosopher mentioned in his

texts. Does this suggest that he is untrue to his method or is there some way in which criticism can be developed along Hegelian lines? In the Preface to the *Phenomenology* Hegel advises the would be critic that only by grasping each standpoint on its own terms and rigorously pursuing its 'inner necessity' can one put a philosophy to the test: the transcendence of a philosophical system must be:

> derived and developed from the nature of the principle itself, and is not just accomplished by bringing in from elsewhere counter assurances and chance fancies. (PG.MM.27/B.85)

There is here a suggestion that the transcendence of a shape of consciousness is inevitable, which reveals that for Hegel the shapes of consciousness described and the cultures they reflect are dynamic and liable to break into self-contradiction. In the following chapter we shall consider the possibilities of a critical interpretation of Hegel before assessing the relevance of Hegel to contemporary philosophy.

NOTES

[1] See T. S. Kuhn, *The Structure of Scientific Revolutions,* Chicago: University Press, 1971.

[2] This, of course, is not to say that philosophy competes with science on its own terms, but that a philosophical investigation might show that what was held to have the hardness of scientific fact in reality rested on confusion.

[3] Kuhn, op. cit, p.94.

[4] S. Kierkegaard, *Purity of Heart,* London: Fontana, 1964. p.47.

[5] R. Bambrough, *Reason, Truth and God*, p.29.

[6] Ibid. pp.29-30.

[7] Ibid. p.135.

[8] A. Kojève, *An Introduction to the Reading of Hegel,* trans. J. H. Nichols Jnr., London: Basic Books Inc., 1969. p.35.

[9] M. Clark, *Logic and System,* The Hague: Martinus Nijhoff, 1971. p.196.

[10] Ibid. p.209.

[11] Kojève, op. cit, p.x.

12] I. Soll, *An Introduction to Hegel's Metaphysics,* Chicago: University Press, 1975. pp.102-3.

13] Kuhn, op. cit, pp.140-1.

14] A. R. Manser, *Hegel's Logic,* Philosophy Department Notes: University of Southampton, 1971.

15] Ibid.

16] Ibid.

17] B. Russell, *My Philosophical Development,* London: Allen and Unwin, 1959. p.216.

18] Ibid. p.230.

19] J. M. E. McTaggart, *Studies in the Hegelian Dialectic,* Cambridge: University Press, 1896. pp.203-4.

20] Ibid. p.204.

21] J. L. Stocks, *Morality and Purpose,* London: Routledge, 1969. p.29.

22] Whilst Hegel combatted the objectification of truth from within philosophy, Marx saw objectification as a phenomenon relative to a specific historic period and sought to abolish philosophy by revolutionary changes in the economic structure. Although Hegel recognised the important connections between economic activity and social life in general (See PR.244-8) he would have argued that the economic structure was too narrow a foundation for the entire edifice of philosophical estrangement. In his *Studies on Marx and Hegel,* Hyppolite asks: 'Is there not in love, in human relations, in the mutual recognition of men, in technology by means of which man creates and builds the world, and in the political administration of the State, even where socialist, a representation of the self external to itself through the Other which presupposes a kind of separation or alienation which one may continually seek to displace but which forever subsists and is consequently part of the very notion of the Absolute that is open to man?' (*Studies in Marx and Hegel,* edited and translated by John O'Neill, London: Heinemann, 1961. p.87) For Hegel, objectification and estrangement appear to be part of the human condition, whereas for Marx there is a solution in the coming revolution.

[23] See Gustav Emil Müller, 'Interdependence of *Phenomenology, Logic* and *Encyclopaedia*', in *New Studies in Hegel's Philosophy*, edited by W. E. Steinkraus, New York: Holt, Rinehart and Winston, 197C p.20.

[24] See W. Kaufmann, *Hegel: A Reinterpretation, Texts and Commentar* London: Weidenfeld & Nicolson, 1966. pp.111-2, for an account c the publication details of the *Phenomenology*. Also see 'Hegel's Concept of Phenomenology' by Kaufmann, in *Phenomenology and Phil sophical Understanding*, edited by Edo Pivcevic, Cambridge: University Press, 1975. pp.211-230, for an account of Hegel's chan- ging views on the *Phenomenology*.

[25] Kaufmann, *Hegel: A Reinterpretation, Texts and Commentary*, p.14

[26] Ibid. p.156.

[27] The reference to McTaggart here is from *A Commentary on Hegel's Logic*, London, 1910, where it is said that: 'The dialectical pr cess of the *Logic* is an absolutely essential element in Hegel's system. If we accepted this and rejected everything else that Hegel had written, we should have a system of philosophy'. p.2.

[28] *Hegel: A Reinterpretation, Texts and Commentary*, p.172.

[29] *Brief von und an Hegel*, edited by J. H. Hoffmeister, Hamburg, 19 1,145,161,200.

[30] 'Yet in the fall of 1831 Hegel began preparations for a second edition of the *Phenomenology* and made a note for himself reading "Unusual early work, not to be revised"'. J. Habermas, *Knowledg and Human Interests*, translated by J. Shapiro, London: Heineman 1972. p.23.

[31] Kaufmann, 'Hegel's Ideas About Tragedy' in *New Studies in Hegel' Philosophy*. pp.215-6.

[32] Otto Pöggeler 'Die Komposition der *Phänomenologie des Geistes*' in *Materialen zu Hegel's Phänomenologie des Geistes*, edited by Fulda and Heinrich, Frankfurt am Main, 1973.

[33] Pöggeler, op. cit, p.34.

[34] 'Aber Hegel muss irgendwann die Herrschaft über seine Arbeit veloren haben: das fünfte Kapitel "Gewissheit und Wahrheit über Vernunft" ist unpoportioneert lang - 214 Seiten des ersten Kapitels'. Pöggeler, op. cit, p.350.

35] Müller, *New Studies in Hegel's Philosophy,* p.21.

36] Ibid. p.20.

37] See Hegel, 'the arrangements of the planets in space is the act of the planets themselves'. (Enz. II. 280).

38] St. Augustine, *Confessions,* xii,i. See Wittgenstein's *Zettel* 457, which the editors translate as 'because the search says more than the discovery'.

39] The reference to G. Pitcher's *The Philosophy of Wittgenstein,* Englewood Cliffs, NJ: Prentice Hall Inc., 1964, and the quotation is taken from a review article by Rush Rhees in *Discussions of Wittgenstein,* p.42. My use of this quotation, and the example given, should not be taken as an indication of any support for the 'two Wittgenstein' thesis anymore than it should lend support to the notion that there is no meaningful difference between the *Tractatus* and the *Investigations.* The point is that it does not make any sense to look for a yardstick against which one can judge each work. Hegel's metaphor of the bud and the blossom is applicable here, since we can see Wittgenstein's later writings as a development out of the former - despite Wittgenstein's belief that he was, in his later work, destroying all that had gone before.

V Hegel and modern philosophy

1. THE CRITICAL ELEMENT IN DESCRIPTION

You don't need a weatherman to know which way the wind blows.
[Bob Dylan]

Hegel's insistence that philosophy must be descriptive has lent suppor
to the view that his philosophy is conservative, a justification of th
existing order. His political philosophy is often interpreted as a de
ification of the Prussian state and an unkind critic once said of the
Philosophy of Right, that it was 'grown on the dunghills of servility;
not in the garden of science'. Similar accusations can be made agains
any philosophy which does not see itself as a means of providing blue-
prints for the future society. Wittgenstein's notorious dictum: 'The
game is played' has similarly been criticised for its explicit conservatism and parallels have been drawn by W. H. Walsh between Wittgenstein's respect for accepted institutions and Burke's respect for the
ancien régime.[1] But just as there is a left-wing and radical interpre
tation of Hegel, represented by Marx and Engels, so there is also a
growing awareness of the possibility of an alignment between certain
strands of Wittgenstein's thought and the Marxian concept of *praxis.*[2]
In what follows we shall indicate the nature of both Hegel and Wittgen
stein's critical standpoint, beginning with a consideration of the typ
of examples which might be employed to demonstrate the alleged conservatism of the claim that a language game or shape of consciousness is
order as it is.

a. Wittgenstein's appeal to rules, to the way the game is played, len
support to a conservative interpretation wherein appeals to tradition
rule out the possibility of new and revolutionary language games. In
analysis of the concept of 'political authority' Peter Winch draws att
tion to an affinity between Wittgenstein's concept of 'following a rul
and following the rules laid down by legitimately established politica
authorities.[3] The meaningfulness of political concepts and political
objectives is thus anchored to established traditions.[4] Like Hegel,
Winch maintains that political objectives are meaningful only against
the background of a system of established institutions and rules. The
teachings of Christ, however revolutionary, can only be understood
against the background of the Jewish tradition; a Pope cannot 'issue a
Encyclical denying the existence of God, and advocate the practice of
free love and still maintain papal authority with it.'[5] The weight of
tradition, it would appear, rests 'like a nightmare upon the brain of
the living'. A total rupture in the historic continuum, as envisaged
by many Marxists, would appear to be logically impossible. It is inde
difficult on these terms to see how one can ever break with establishe
traditions. The possibility of a conservative interpretation of Wittgenstein is indeed apparent and this, no doubt, is what lies behind

Walsh's comparison of Wittgenstein to Burke. Yet whilst Marx and the left-Hegelians spoke of a revolutionary break with all existing traditions they were like the Wittgensteinians, fully aware of the logical difficulties involved in the attempt to postulate blue-prints for the post-revolutionary society, insisting that the political and social objectives of the revolutionary society would have to be determined by the new order, not by the utopian planners of the present epoch. For those who believe that philosophy should provide blue-prints for the future society often forget that its object will be very much determined by the needs of the present society. Given that a future society could well have different objectives, we could well find that the blue-prints are more of an impediment than a means of realising objectives.

Winch is fully aware that political objectives are determined by the present epoch and speaks of the British Labour Party's commitment to nationalization as an example of political objectives being justified by appeals to tradition. But what is interesting philosophically is the way in which demands are thrown up independent of the established arena of political discourse. Nationalization has quite a long ancestry in European politics, and had long been recuperated within a capitalist economic system. But the demands of workers in the 1968 movement for *autogestion* revealed a rejection of the manifestoes of conservatives, social-democrats and allegedly revolutionary-communist parties alike. When traditional ritualistic slogans about nationalization were replaced with demands for *autogestion* into what tradition had the workers delved? Lucien Goldmann draws attention to the extraordinary degree of spontaneity in the demand for *autogestion*.

> In the West, despite the confusions and the traditional forms of thought and of language which prevent them from becoming fully conscious of their own actions, the new socialist forces have shown themselves developed to an extraordinary scale and possessed of an extraordinary spontaneity. In two weeks the concept of *autogestion* which only existed in a few books and was known only by a few thousand intellectuals, had penetrated, if only as a possibility and as a problem, into the consciousness of millions of workers and of students.[6]

It was not until such demands were recuperated, when *autogestion* was replaced with 'workers' control' or even worse 'workers' participation',[7] that a tradition became available for the purpose of explaining what was considered inexplicable at the time. As is the case with many historical facts, traditions tell us as much about the present as they do about the past. After 1968 all the traditional parties and sects re-emerged with explanations that all the workers had demanded was, after all, in their own party programmes all the time. This, of course, is to draw attention to the familiar point that revolutionaries are always

107

overtaken by the revolutions they later claim to have initiated, why one of the greatest impediments to revolutionary change is often, para doxically, the revolutionaries themselves. Trapped within the traditions of previous revolutions, their objectives and strategies, they are too often incapable of seeing the revolution before their eyes. Ar when it takes place they can impose meaning upon it only by invoking the ghost of past revolutions. Like military strategists who are always ready for the last war, revolutionaries are always prepared to re-enact their glorious history. And once it becomes possible to harness the forces of the revolution, and impose upon it objectives derived from the past, then is the split with the traditional order healec In a very important sense the successful revolutionary, whose objectives are formulated within the old order, functions towards the retur of the movement to existing traditions. In the event of a radical break with existing tradition, then the revolution will, if necessary, create new traditions to look back upon. Traditions can be defined re trospectively and do not weigh as heavily upon the brain of the living as a Burkean interpretation of Wittgenstein would suggest. Because th fit between words and reality is never complete, traditions can be invoked to explain some of the most radical breaches with established practices.

b. Advancing a Wittgensteinian philosophy of religion, D. Z. Phillips makes the following observations about the practice of child sacrifice

> Certainly, we often condemn those who hold moral opinions which are different from our own. We say they are wrong in holding such views. But when the views and actions in question are tied up with a culture different from our own, the position is altered. If I hear that one of my neighbours has killed another neighbour's child, given that he is sane, my condemnation is immediate...But if I hear that some remote tribe practices child sacrifice, what then? I do not know what sacrifice means for the tribe in question. What would it mean to say I condemned it when the 'it' refers to something I know nothing about? If I did condemn it I would be condemning murder. But murder is not child sacrifice. 'The ethical expression of Abraham's action is that he wished to murder Isaac: the religious expression is that he wished to sacrifice him'.[8]

It is obvious that whilst Phillips is rejecting an appeal to any trans cendental absolute, he is not making out a case in favour of infanticide or child sacrifice. Yet this passage might be interpreted as an example of Wittgensteinian conservatism, so conservative that on Wittgenstein's terms there is no possibility of criticising the reprehensible practice of child-sacrifice in either some remote tribe or Biblical past. The game is played. What is murder in one language game is only sacrifice in another and neither game can produce a standard for criticising the other, just as the soccer rule-book cannot be employed to criticise what happens on the snooker table. This, of course, is a misrepresentation of Wittgenstein's descriptive method. In fact a more complete description of the social background to the above-mentioned practices should provide sufficient ammunition for criticism. The example of the child-sacrificers, like Wittgenstein's wood-sellers, is, as it stands, abstract and one-sided. If we know nothing about a society we cannot, as Phillips says, condemn their practices without knowing what they mean to them. But all we know of the sacrificers is that they sacrifice. The correct reply to a philosopher who cites examples of such practices, adding 'and this is proper in their society', is to demand more information. This is what one should do when presented with Wittgenstein's 'imaginary tribes'. Can they really go on in the way they are presented? With a little more information about their society, one would discover - certainly in real societies - that such practices are far from being universally accepted and their meaning very different to different members of that society.

One of the problems here is that Wittgenstein never described real societies. This is one of his shortcomings and as such his lack of a sense of historical significance robs his work of the vitality that is found in Hegel's descriptive approach. This is rather unfortunate because it encourages a relativistic tendency to imagine all kinds of wierd practices in isolation from their social context and put them forward as examples of possible language games. But in the case of the sacrificers it is very clear that any society in which child sacrifice was performed would have, within it, considerable opposition to the practice and to those institutions which stood to gain something from it. In actual societies where human sacrifice has existed the speed with which they succumbed to European colonialists who outlawed such activities, reveals that the meaning they attributed to human sacrifice was remarkably close to that held by the Europeans.

The second example in the passage quoted from Phillips refers to Kierkegaard's distinction between murder and sacrifice with an appeal to Abraham's attempted sacrifice of his son, Isaac. We do, however, possess considerable knowledge about the social and religious background to this example. It is, in fact, an important part of the religious tradition held throughout Europe and the Western world for the past two thousand years. But this tradition has rarely, if ever, excused child sacrifice on any grounds. This language game is not allowed. As we have argued in chapter one, there are definite limits governing the acceptability of certain language games. The practice of child sacrifice could, if actually performed, be cited as evidence for the abolition of the religious game in which it is played. Had the Mormons not restricted their beliefs in polygamy it is doubtful whether the Mormon religion would have been tolerated. A religion which advocated actual sacrifice, instead of mere tales of sacrifice, would attract very few believers and could only sustain itself by force. Moreover, it is not at all clear that one can redescribe the killing of one's son in such a way as to make it less reprehensible. Merely because Kierkegaard can invoke a religious language game in which the term 'sacrifice' can replace 'infanticide' cannot provide justification for the initial outrage. It can indicate a further dimension of moral corruption. When the Pentagon described the massacre of a Vietnamese village as 'Personnel wastage' the use of a bureaucratic language game served only to intensify moral repugnance, since a more sinister aspect of the initial crime was revealed in the way that language was distorted to conceal reality. Religion has no more right to exonerate infanticide by calling it 'sacrifice' than a bureaucratic war machine can exonerate genocide by calling it 'personnel wastage'.

How strong was the adherence to human sacrifice in the society of Abraham? We know that Abraham had a 'world-view' which included a jealous God, whose instructions had to be obeyed, so he resolved to kill his son when ordered. We also know that the boy and his mother worshipped the same God as Abraham. Yet we also know that Isaac and his mother would not have approved of Abraham's intentions since the latter went to considerable lengths to conceal the identity of the sacrificial 'victim' from them. We might not be able to classify Abraham as a psychopath without bringing in the psychology of the last two centuries to bear on the issue, but we can say that he was a liar on his own terms. We can also say that the intended slaying of his son was immoral, from the point of view of the mother and son - who shared the same culture - and probably illegal, since Abraham took pains to deceive them. We know, furthermore, that there were religious objections to deceit, and probably similar objections to unauthorised sacrifice. In this story Abraham is clearly out of step with the rest of his society. But, it must be emphasised, the Abraham story is *meant* as a story, not as an historical account. It is a story designed to dramatise man's relationship to an all-powerful God. As such the kind of questions that would be pertinent in the real world can safely be brushed aside, having no relevance to the point of the story. In the real world Abraham would have to decide whether child sacrifice on God's orders can be carried out without violating other divine imperatives. In the real world he would either have been prevented from carrying out his intentions or be classified as a criminal or lunatic. That a God can make his wishes known to individuals, says Hegel, 'may only be admitted *in abstracto*, but not in actuality, and it is believed in no individual cases. Men do not believe that to him, to this individual, there has been a revelation. For why to him more than to others?' (GP.1.MM.500/H.433)

As previously remarked, Wittgenstein did not concern himself with the specific conditions of his imaginative examples, which is why it is empting to see his imaginary tribes as fully-integrated societies. But one of Hegel's important contributions to philosophy is the argument that a society must have contradictions; that there must be a play in the gearing between language and human practices, and that the fully-integrated society has never existed. If it did exist it would exhibit no confusions, no grounds for philosophical puzzlement, or possibility for new ideas. It would remain static, like those model societies exhibited in museums. So whilst Hegel's approach is descriptive, it is also developmental; the shapes of consciousness described in the *Phenomenology* reflect a built-in feature of dynamic growth, an ability to change and absorb concepts from other societies, thus generating contradictions. In an important respect Hegel's method is more descriptive than the Wittgensteinian approach since the former insists that a shape of consciousness must be examined in its historic and social setting. We, the phenomenological observers, are invited to observe the relationship between the shape - or 'world-view' - and the way of life in which it emerges. This, argues Hegel, involves no contribution from us, since we can accept that shape's own account of the social reality as a truth. All that we must do is observe whether the shape in question can give an adequate account of its social reality.

2. Let us now consider how Hegel examines a world-view and its relation to reality in the *Phenomenology*. In the chapter entitled 'Self-consciousness', Hegel portrays a Stoic consciousness which has emerged from the master-servant confrontation. Whilst the master-servant dialectic ends with Hegel's account of how, through the knowledge acquired in working upon the natural world, the slave comes to achieve the upper hand, the attention of the reader is directed towards the slave who accepts the condition of slavery and provides a rationalisation for his servitude. The Stoic consciousness, thus depicted, is one wherein the social fact of slavery is not disputed. Everyone within that form of life recognises the existence of slaves, although some may approve or disapprove. But let us consider the account of slavery and its opposite, freedom, which emerges from the Stoic consciousness. For the Stoic, thought and action are abstractly opposed. Freedom is to be found within the faculty of thought and can be comprehended in isolation from the social world. To think is to be free from the master. He may control the movements of my limbs but at least my mind is free. How true is this? Can anyone think as he pleases in total independence of his social relationships? How private, how peculiar, are the individual's thoughts? The key assumption which Hegel locates in Stoicism is that thought is arbitrary. The Stoic is presented as one who allows thought to have no restrictions. Stoicism is heavily subjective, even to the point of claiming that values have no public relevance.

Against the Stoic, Hegel points out that to speak of freedom without any reference to the ability to live a life of freedom is mere word play. As Loewenberg puts it: 'A world where a Marcus Aurelius and an

Epictetus are alleged to be co-equal in the enjoyment of abstract free
dom is a world running its course heedless of such innocuous equality
Says Hegel:

> the essence of this consciousness is to be free, on the throne
> or in fetters, throughout all the dependence that attaches to
> its individual existence, and to maintain that solid lifeless
> unconcern which persistently withdraws from the movement of
> existence, from effective *activity* as well as from passive
> endurance, into the simple essentiality of thought. (PG.MM.157/
> B.244)

Marx was probably closer to Hegel than he would admit when he wrote
that:

> 'Liberation' is an historical and not a mental act, and it is
> brought about by historical conditions, the development of
> industry, commerce, agriculture, the conditions of intercourse...

Just as action involves choices, preferences, moral dilemmas and remo
the complete detachment of Stoic thought, which paralyses action, is
tantamount to moral abdication. The equation between goodness and
passive thought is itself a denial of morality. Limited to the mere
use of general terms like 'true', 'just' and so on, but prohibited fr
applying them in any actual situation, the Stoic can do nothing virtuous. Stoicism might be held as an 'abstract principle' but it cann
stand as a moral code which works in any actual society. He who limi
his conduct to the utterance of a few elevating terms without the dee
to back them up, 'soon begins to get wearysome'. (PG.MM.159/B.246) Th
Stoic, with his talk of abstract freedom, is at best a boring chatter
box and at worst an apologist for the powers that be.

The one-sidedness of the Stoic consciousness is revealed by taking
claim to possess freedom seriously. Given that the institution of
slavery existed, we are spared the search for evidence of slave rebel
lions to refute the Stoic consciousness; we find epistemological confusion in the claim that 'man is free on the throne or in fetters'.
Hegel simply requests that the Stoic describes his freedom, but warns
him not to use words which can only have a meaning against the background of a life where freedom could be actively realised. Epictetus
cannot. Freedom as envisaged by the Stoic, turns out to be a form of
self-deceit. His language, parasitic upon the language of men who
enjoy the freedom denied to him, refutes him. Yet in drawing attenti
to this fact Hegel has employed no principle of his own, save the
demand that the Stoic be consistent in his arguments.

d. In the above example, Stoicism is overcome by its own inherent
logical weakness. But Hegel's descriptive approach is not confined to
pointing out logical confusion. Operating with a dynamic conception
of social existence one can describe the forces at work within a form
of social life which will in turn generate a new standard of social
criticism. A good example here is Hegel's account of the contradictions within Civil Society in the *Philosophy of Right*. Describing the
tendency towards over-production in Civil Society, Hegel concludes that
on its own terms it soon 'becomes apparent that despite an excess of
wealth Civil Society is not rich enough...to check excessive poverty
and the creation of a penurious rabble'. (PR.245) The alternatives,
says Hegel, would violate the essential principles of Civil Society.
For example, should the burden of maintaining the unemployed be placed
on the shoulders of the wealthy it would violate the belief that an individual should provide for himself by his work and lead to further vio-
lations of related concepts like 'independence', 'self-respect' and so
on. On the other hand the creation of subsidised work schemes would
only lead to further over-production and thus exacerbate the problem.
Unwilling to accept either alternative Civil Society is obliged to
accept a third alternative: colonialisation and the expansion of its
markets overseas with the consequent problems entailed.

> This inner dialectic of Civil Society thus drives it - or at
> any rate drives a specific Civil Society - to push beyond its
> own limits and seek markets, and so its necessary means of
> subsistence, in other lands which are either deficient in the
> goods it has over-produced, or else generally backward in
> industry, etc. (PR.246)

Written almost one hundred years before Lenin's *Imperialism: The
Highest Stage of Capitalism,* Hegel's description of the internal dia-
lectic of Civil Society was to provide the intellectual tools for the
Marxist critique of the events leading up to the first World War.

e. Under the influence of Hegel, the early Marx adopted a method of
taking seriously the unquestioned assumptions of nineteenth-century
political economy in order to demonstrate how it frustrates its own
objectives. In the *Economic and Philosophical Manuscripts of 1844*
he says:

> We started from the presuppositions of political economy. We
> accepted its vocabulary and its laws. We presupposed private
> property, the separation of labour, capital and land, and like-
> wise of wages, profit and ground rent; also division of labour;
> competition; the concept of exchange value etc. Using the very
> words of political economy we have demonstrated how the worker
> is degraded to the most miserable sort of commodity; that the
> misery of the worker is in inverse proportion to the power and

113

size of his production; that the necessary result of competition
is the accumulation of power in a few hands, and thus a more
terrible restoration of monopoly; and that finally the distinction between capitalist and landlord, and that between peasant
and industrial worker disappears and the whole of society must
fall apart into two classes of the property owners and the
propertyless workers.[11]

Using none other than the language appropriate to the shape of conscio
ness being described Marx's critique proceeds immanently towards an
account of a society polarised by class conflict. The unquestioned
assumption of political economy that Marx seizes upon is 'the fact of
private property'. 'Political economy', he says, 'starts with the fac
of private property, it does not explain it to us'.[12] For Marx, the
foundations of political economy were bound up with the interests of
property owners. Hence: 'the interest of the capitalist is the ultimate court of appeal'.[13] It may be the case that these interests conflict with those of the labouring classes but Marx's point is that the
framework of intelligibility was governed by the assumptions concernin
private property, to question them would be to step outside of what wa
then considered to be rational discourse. And this was Marx's point:
the limits of rational discourse, thus drawn, were one-sided and incom
plete. A total picture of the society depicted by political economy
must take into consideration the interests of other classes than the
property owners. To take the assumptions of political economy serious
to draw out what is implicitly in them, is to see the implications for
the labouring classes. Moreover, if Marx were correct in drawing out
the implications of political economy the system he described was
characterised by a severance of knowledge from reality, heading rapid]
towards acute crisis.

Wittgenstein's injunction not to think, but to look at the way the
various language games are played, and Hegel's exhortation to 'make nc
contribution' but simply observe the succession of shapes does not mea
that each language game or shape of consciousness is beyond criticism.
If this were so then any claim to have given expression to absolute
truth would have equal validity with others. Each *in itself* is to be
criticised according to its own standard. This often involves taking
the standard more seriously than its original exponent may have intended. Hegel's method involves taking the philosopher at his word and
applying his principles rigidly. The analogy with Wittgenstein is vel
strong here. Both are opposed to the reification or thought which has
its origin in a fascination with a one-sided picture, and the method
employed to overcome this consists in returning concepts to their soc
context. Commenting on Wittgenstein's 'To imagine a language is to

imagine a form of life' (PI.19), Strawson's interpretation of Wittgenstein's method could well serve as an introduction to Hegel:

> to understand a concept, a word, put the word in the linguistic context and the whole utterance in its social context and then describe, without preoccupation, what you find; remembering that each word, each utterance, may figure in *many* contexts.[14]

Making only a slight alteration to Strawson's text we could describe Hegel's method as follows: to understand what is wrong with a philosophical position requires that we put the concepts it uses in a linguistic and social setting and then describe, without preoccupations, the social and linguistic changes necessary to give these concepts any meaning. In short, take the philosopher seriously and imagine that the world is exactly how it is depicted by him. Neither Hegel nor Wittgenstein saw philosophy's role as providing refutations of scientific or sociological truths, but on the contrary by drawing out from the accepted accounts of these 'truths' the fact that they are abstract and one-sided distortions of the reality they are held to depict. Although philosophy is descriptive it does not 'leave everything as it is'. On this point Rush Rhees' remarks about Wittgenstein's conception of philosophical inquiry are instructive:

> When Wittgenstein spoke of Hilbert's remark that 'no one shall drive us from the heaven that Cantor has created for us', he said 'I would never dream of trying to drive anyone from any heaven. I would try to do something quite different: to show that it is not heaven. And then you'll leave it on your own accord.'[15]

In the same way psychology has not escaped from either Wittgenstein's or Hegel's criticism of its fundamental notions; the life sciences have been transformed by philosophical criticism of rigidly drawn antinomies between mechanism and vitalism, and the social sciences have not been unaffected by both Hegelian and Wittgensteinian critiques of positivism.

2. PROFESSIONAL PHILOSOPHY

> Philosophical problems arise when language goes on holiday.
> [Wittgenstein (PI.38)]

Hegel differs from many other philosophers in the value he attributes to philosophy in the range of human experience. For this reason he is closer to the Greeks than any other philosopher of the modern period. Philosophy, for Hegel, is supreme, penetrating every branch of knowledge. He would therefore find himself in opposition to the contemporary trend within Anglo-Saxon circles which sees philosophy as a specialist profession not concerned with problems arising in other disciplines. Accordingly, philosophy is seen as one more profession amongst others, 'a subject which' says G. J. Warnock, 'its practitioners should be left to practise'[16] As a specialist activity philosophy is comparatively insignificant. Says Warnock:

> There is not, I believe, any serious doubt that among the many forces which tend to shape and modify the prevailing beliefs and attitudes of societies, the influence of philosophers has been exceedingly small, and on any view is certain to remain so. Philosophers are less numerous than the clergy, less intelligible than the novelists, less exciting than political pamphleteers, less revered than scientists. A philosopher who leaves the beliefs of the public alone need not fear that those questions will cease to be pursued and publicised, nor perhaps could he hope for much success if he should enter that arena.[17]

Hegel would find the above argument unintelligible, although he would agree with the contemporary opinion that philosophy cannot borrow its standards from other disciplines. But Hegel's reason is that it is precisely because of the elevated position philosophy enjoys in relation to other disciplines that it cannot employ the standards of mathematics, the empirical sciences, art, religion, or even common-sense. There is, however, much in Hegel's conception that is acceptable to modern philosophers. It is widely accepted that the object of philosophy differs from the objects of the other sciences in the wa that the interests of a philosopher can focus equally on the method and on the content. But many modern Anglo-Saxon philosophers would disavow the status which Hegel bestowed upon philosophy. The absence of any external standard for the assessment of a philosophical system, the absence of any concrete results, or specific end product, has led to the assumption that philosophy is an insignificant pursuit. In the above quotation, it is clear that Warnock himself is operating with a utilitarian criterion as to the importance of philosophy in the plan of human experience. From a utilitarian view philosophy can appear to be either trivial or meaningless. Since there are no external checks on philosophical language, except those employed within philosophy, it seems that philosophy is relatively trivial; a harmless game that cannot yield any definite knowledge about the world but can have the bene ficial effect of sharpening one's wits. According to one critic of contemporary English philosophy its contribution is indirect, its problems exist only to provide intellectual training for a future ruling class.[18]

On the other hand there is a point of view, derived from a Wittgensteinian concept of language, which argues that philosophy is not a genuine activity at all. This standpoint opposes the belief that

philosophy is a genuine 'profession' but relatively insignificant, because it accepts a thesis, close to Hegel's, that unlike the other
sciences philosophy has no object of study other than itself. For
Wittgenstein philosophy is nonsensical but paradoxically he wants to
say that it is also important. He is prevented from asserting its
importance, prevented from answering its questions, because his theory
of language excludes any meaningful usage for the propositions of
philosophy. The latter, he insists, is parasitic on other 'language-
games' and cannot be seen as a genuine language-game in itself.

Both schools have one important factor in common: their hostility
towards Hegel and an acceptance of Russell's assurance that 'almost all
of Hegel's doctrines are false'. Against the followers of Wittgenstein,
Hegel would argue that philosophy is a genuine subject capable of solving its own problems. But he would not agree that it is a specialist
or trivial activity. Yet whilst he shares with Wittgenstein and his
followers the view that philosophy is generated within the various
sciences, whilst having no specific content of its own, he is not committed to their conclusion that philosophy is unreal, the result of
accidents within the various spheres of knowledge. On the contrary,
the very absence of a specific content provides Hegel with grounds for
elevating philosophy above the sciences, since it penetrates human
existence at every level. The presence of philosophy testifies to the
health of the human organism, not its sickness.

It appears that similar assumptions concerning the nature and content
of philosophy reveal antithetical conclusions about its status. Its
shifting status since Hegel's time can be explained with reference to
the growth of professionalism and the development of philosophy as a
separate academic subject: a process which became apparent when philosophers began to publish their work in professional journals. By the
turn of the century philosophy had become a recognised profession. Unlike the works of Bradley and Mill, the works of Russell and Moore were
published in professional journals. But professional philosophy,
written for philosophers, has a limited market. Producing papers for
each other's consumption the activity of professional philosophers resembles the work of the islanders who make their living by taking in
each other's washing. Such an economic system cannot exist in the real
world and left to itself professional philosophy would wither away.
Unlike the legal profession which can extort large fees from its clients
as new avenues for litigation open up, professional philosophers are
obliged to rely upon the generosity of the authorities, and those prepared to finance their teaching and research. The survival of philosophy as a profession is very much dependent upon not biting the hand
that feeds it. But philosophers rarely show such tendencies and,
being a somewhat cautious bunch, manage to keep trouble-makers and
dissidents out of the profession. A curious combination of an instinct

117

for self-preservation and desire for professional status and integrity lies behind the present quietism and passivity of contemporary Anglo-Saxon philosophy. For this reason the powerful political and economic forces of the day do not find it necessary to threaten philosophers with the big stick, (and consequently many analytic philosophers are prone to see nought but linguistic confusion in the suggestion that there is a big stick) since the acquisition of professional status necessitates a devitalisation of the subject and a dilution of its social criticism. A professional needs to have a precise knowledge of his sphere of interest and the boundaries require a clear demarcation. The bulk of theology, for example, can be left to the theologians, science and politics to the scientists and politicians. With the exception of certain logical studies it is difficult to see what remains for the professional philosopher. It is not difficult to see how, in this process, philosophy comes to be seen as an interesting but relatively insignificant profession. Its trivialisation through specialisation reflects the contemporary rationalisation of society into atomistic units, with the unit of philosophy having the appearance of frivolity. Ironically the philosopher who trivialises his subject-matter is the true representative of a bureaucratically divided culture.

The professionalisation of philosophy and its concomitant trivialisation is not simply an outcome of the fact that it is taught in educational establishments, as one subject amongst other fields of interest. Socrates and the sophists earned their living from teaching philosophy. So did Kant and Hegel, and Descartes too, found employmen at the Swedish court without being a professional in the above sense. Professionalism is not determined by conditions of employment but by a particular attitude towards philosophy. Professionalism begins when philosophy is treated as a subject that can be distinguished clearly, by means of an attested procedure, from other aspects of human life. For the professional there are clearly defined limits to philosophical inquiry. Their existence enables him to avoid certain uncomfortable channels of thought with phrases like 'This may be interesting but the philosophical issue is so and so'. For the professional, philosophy is an activity like chess, which one can engage in if one so desires; its players can agree upon a set of rules and procedures for changing them should difficulties occur. Like problems in chess its problems d not have a great deal of relevance in the outside world. Dedicated philosophers, like dedicated chess players, will show indignation towa fellow players who introduce political and social problems into the ga Indeed the introduction of politics into sport - a lament of those who oppose calls for the boycotting of sports fixtures with totalitarian regimes - is seen as a corruption of the practice in much the same way as the authors of the 'Gould Report' view the introduction of a political and social content into philosophical inquiry.[19] Against bo

118

it is necessary to point out that politics has always had a prominent place in the sporting fixtures of totalitari n societies from Hitler and Stalin's dictatorships to the present regimes of South Africa and Chile. Similarly, politics has never been far from the surface in philosophical circles, though of late it has been the politics of passivity and surrender to the powerful political forces of the day. For the quietist professional, however, a good philosopher is like a good sportsman: as long as he leaves the public alone he need not fear that his questions will cease to be pursued.

In this way we arrive at an arbitrary limit imposed on philosophy: undemonstrated assumptions concerning what the public will or will not tolerate, which are employed as a conservative base from which the scope of philosophy can be limited. Like any other limits on philosophical discourse, they presuppose a consensus that may not exist. Which section of the public might be outraged? And what of the philosopher who measures his success by the extent to which he outrages certain members of the public? Who is correct? To what transcendental rule book does one appeal?

Although many would disagree, Wittgenstein must be understood against this back-cloth. Above all else, Wittgenstein was a professional - a philosopher's philosopher. Yet paradoxically an aspect of his work embraces Hegel's view that philosophy is intimately bound up with the important matters in human life and, for this reason, can neither be trivial nor the subject of specialist inquiries. This aspect of his work is glossed over by many of his disciples with vague mumblings concerning that which 'runs deep in our lives', lest it awaken the metaphysical dragons they claim to have slain with the master's technique. But in spite of their lip service to the importance of philosophy and a patronising attitude towards the urge to run against the limits of language, the work of Wittgenstein and his disciples has contributed to the contemporary trivialisation of the subject. Both Hegel and Wittgenstein represent a turning away from traditional ways of seeing philosophy as an abstract enterprise concerned with the discovery and examination of foundational truths upon which the edifice of language and knowledge are said to rest. Instead they exhort the reader to put away his critical blinkers and examine the richness of language and experience in all its multifarious forms of expression. But unlike Hegel, Wittgenstein never fully disassociated himself from the critical attempt of the *Tractatus* to isolate the philosophical content of experience from other branches of knowledge. Whilst his later works reject the notion of a once and for all critique of language and knowledge, he still maintained a dividing line between philosophy and other branches of knowledge which he drew in terms of a utilitarian account of language. Consequently he lent encouragement to the tendency to evaluate philosophical discourse according to utilitarian standards.

3. THE USEFULNESS OF PHILOSOPHY

> The confusions which occupy us arise when language is like an engine idling, not when it is doing work. [Wittgenstein PI.132]

To use Wittgenstein's terminology philosophy is one subject that cannot lay claim to be a genuine language game. According to this view philosophy has its origins in a confusion in language, from a failure to discern subtleties between 'depth' and 'surface' grammar, arising when language 'goes on holiday', when the 'machinery of language is idling'. It is a queer activity, having no genuine subject-matter of its own, unlike the other sciences where something useful is done. Philosophy, one might continue, can advance no theses, can answer no questions, because, as a matter of fact, there are no genuine questions in philosophy (See PI. 38, 90, 91, 109, 123, 132, 194, 309, 593).

This view can be expressed in terms of the following analogy: imagine a machine where the cows go in at one end and sausages emerge from the other end. The appropriate science appertaining to this process would have the machine as its object. It would involve an understanding of how it transforms the cows into sausages, how efficiently it does this, and so on. But now consider another machine where the cows go in at one end only to re-emerge as cows at the other end. The machine whirrs and clicks, the lights go on and off, but no transformation of the cows has taken place, nor is any additional information about the cows derived from the machine. Surprisingly there is a science devoted to the study of this 'idle' machine. This science also has a long history, longer, in fact, than most of the other sciences. Generations of men have devoted time and effort to the writing of books and publishing papers about this 'idle' process, and have engaged in many unseemly disputes with each other. Religious and political institutions have occasionally denounced and suppressed the students of this machine but, unlike the efforts of the genuine sausage-makers, their efforts have been recorded by posterity amongst the outstanding achievements of mankind. Everyone has heard of Plato - no one has heard of his sausage-maker.

Now this may seem very puzzling to the outsider. If he is of a strong utilitarian character he might point out that it serves no useful purpose, since the machinery is idling. (It is likely however, that the majority of men would pause and wonder at the machine - a hint of a distinction between the 'ordinary man' and his anti-philosophical 'representative'.) From a utilitarian standpoint the language of philosophy is like the language of the 'idle' machine; what is needed is that the philosopher recognise that his so-called 'science' is based on a misunderstanding of the correct use of the machine. If all the nuts and bolts are tightened up, and if the gears are engaged, the machine will be seen to do a useful task. Likewise, when the 'slackness' is taken out of language philosophical 'idleness' will cease.

Many philosophers who have succumbed to this utilitarian position have sought to establish a logically perfect language free from philosophical slackness. We find this attitude in Brice Parain's attempt to restrict language to a utilitarian function; that of giving and taking orders. Consider Sartre's comment on this endeavour:

> But if we are going to all that trouble to reinvent a language, it must be rigorous and precise. We must eliminate all loose ends and wobbly parts. If the order is to be obeyed it must be understood down to the last details. And conversely, to understand is to act. The belts must be tightened up, the screws driven home. Since we cannot remain silent, that is, cannot directly and immediately attain being, we must at least, rigorously control the intermediaries. Parain admits that in his youth he shuttled back and forth between two dreams. Says Parain, 'Symbols lead us to believe that by eliminating all the transmissions we eliminate all the hitches, and also to believe that, on the other hand, if we perfect all this machinery, the gears will work quite smoothly and accidents will become impossible'.20

Wittgenstein's *Tractatus,* like Kant's *Critique of Pure Reason;* can be seen as an attempt to provide a once and for all critique of language and thought respectively in order to eliminate the kind of slackness that generates speculative metaphysics. The flaw in these attempts lay in the assumption that there was only one genuine function of language and thought. Parain's candidate for the genuine function of language was that of giving orders, an activity which, as we have argued in Chapter II, can only be meaningful if we have a language complete with all its multifarious forms of expression.

Traces of the utilitarian attitude towards the philosophical use of language have nevertheless survived Wittgenstein's *Tractatus* rejection of the attempt to provide a critique of language based on the assumption of its allegedly primary function. In his later works he gave up the idea of postulating the genuine function of language but he still maintained that philosophical accidents - he now spoke of 'diseases' (PI.593) - occur when language breaks loose from its moorings. However, the later work entails the recognition that there is no general remedy for this tendency other than pointing the philosopher back to the correct use of language.21 But despite the much-acclaimed revolutionary breakthrough he still retained a utilitarian attitude towards philosophy, with which his own commitment to its problems was continually to conflict. Philosophy has no place, its problems are unanswerable because they are not genuine problems, he argued. Yet he persisted

with them. It is quite easy to see how philosophers in the wake of
Wittgenstein, but lacking the master's ambivalent attitude towards
philosophy, have applied their efforts to a general debunking of the
subject. In doing so the relative decline in the status of philosophy
is hastened. Those who cannot tear themselves away from the cloisters
to become hospital porters, engineers and other useful functionaries,
seek refuge in the professionalisation of philosophy.

The view that philosophy is an island where all the inhabitants live
by taking in each other's washing, that its problems are trivial, providing only a harmless exercise of the wits, is diametrically opposed
to the Hegelian concept of philosophy solving its own problems. For
the latter, philosophical questions arise within every branch of scienc
calling attention to problems which cannot be solved within the framework of the science in question. But whilst philosophy is of a different order than the sciences the activity of philosophy is not a
trivial pursuit that one can engage in as a form of distraction from
them. Philosophical concepts are not to be employed, says Hegel, to
satisfy a whim, like 'once in a while to see our everyday face be-
daubed with paint: no it is because the method of physics does not
satisfy the concept that we have to go further'. (Enz.II.246.zu)

Facing the argument that philosophy is a trivial pursuit, capable
of solving its own problems as chess can solve its own problems, by
reference to an objective procedure, Hegel would have difficulty in
formulating a reply. We are now dealing with a different concept of
philosophy, a different shape of consciousness. He might reply by
saying that today's professionals are not really doing philosophy, but
conversely they can, and do, reply that Hegel's work was not really
philosophy, but 'amateur science'.

There is, however, an Hegelian reply to the trivialisation of philosophy. It consists in asking 'In what sense are its problems trivial?'
'By what criterion do you judge them to be trivial or pseudo questions?
To Wittgenstein he might add: 'And why are you so concerned with them?
For Wittgenstein philosophical questions are defined as trivial by
means of the criterion operating within every 'language game' that philosophers have transgressed upon. For example, philosophical problems
within the sphere of religion are dissolved by means of appeals to
religious practices, and so on. Accordingly this leaves no scope for
additional philosophical criteria, and so the philosophical dimension
of human experience loses its significance. But in reply to the
assertion that 'philosophy, being a parasitic activity, has no criterio
of its own' Hegel offers his 'for us' - 'for itself'.distinction. Each
shape of consciousness is described from the standpoint internal to it,
and also from the standpoint of the phenomenological observer, who sees
it as one more shape within a developing process-unlike the philosopher
depicted, who sees his work as the completed expression of the

122

absolute. So when faced with the utilitarian account of philosophy the Hegelian can see it as one more shape of 'for itself' amongst others, relative to its historic period. As such it could be replaced by another shape of consciousness. Consider how this might take place. If we present Wittgenstein's objectives on their own terms we find that the genuine solution to philosophical problems lies in the abandonment of philosophy:

> The real discovery is the one that makes one capable of stopping doing philosophy when I want to - The one that gives philosophy peace, so that it is no longer tormented by questions which bring itself into question. (PI.133)

Here Wittgenstein is saying that if we dissolve a philosophical problem it should not lead us into further problems about the method (metaphysics) employed in its dissolution: in short, it should lead to an abandonment of philosophy. According to Wittgenstein this is achieved when we attend to the proper use of the instruments of our speech. Against this view it is necessary to point out that this approach did not satisfy Wittgenstein's desire for peace, nor has it brought an end to philosophy. Moreover, what gives peace to one man may bring torment to another. The Socratic quest for peace disturbed the Athenian order which is why he was put on trial by those who did not think that philosophy was a trivial affair. Remedies for philosophical torment may vary from culture to culture. The Athenians chose hemlock, but it is nowadays fashionable to look towards psycho-analysis and the employment of therapeutic techniques. What must be stressed is the fact that there are no unproblematic solutions to philosophical puzzlement. In psycho-analysis it does not follow that once the patient knows the reasons for his 'abnormal' behaviour he will then cease to behave abnormally; he may decide that his behaviour is correct under the circumstances. Moreover the patient can always claim, often with legitimacy, that the wrong diagnosis has been made, that the analyst is wrong, that his motives and values are dubious. Likewise, in philosophy, one can argue that once philosophy makes the achievement of peace an important objective - insofar as it makes sense to speak of objectives in philosophy - or seeks only to 'leave the public alone', it has already conceded too much to the conservative tendencies of the surrounding culture. Could it not be argued that just as the tools of the psycho-analyst can become a weapon in the hands of an establishment so can a philosophy which has no greater aspiration than rendering the individual at peace by putting an end to the embarrassing questions of philosophers? It may not be fashionable at present to see philosophy as a form of social criticism, but what metaphysical barriers prevent the emergence of a shape of consciousness which makes the above criticism of present philosophy? And if such a critical shape became fashionable who is to say it would be wrong? Operating with a 'for us' - 'for itself' distinction the Hegelian recognises the ultimate relativity of all philosophical standards, including the assumptions that 'peace' can be obtained if philosophy is abandoned for a more useful activity.

The desire for 'peace' may be laudable in the 'darkness of this time'. (PI.viii) And as Wittgenstein lived long enough to have fears of total nuclear destruction he may have shared with his contemporaries the desire for the peace and security of yesterday. It is not surprising that his subversion of philosophy should give rise to the conservative belief that philosophy must be confined to the activity of clarifying conceptual confusion. This position shares with the trivialisation thesis the assumption of metaphysical limits to philosophical enquiry and differs only in the way that it brings into philosophy a certain homeostatic concept of human society and language wherein the ideal state is characteristic of a closed system, rather than a steady state characterised by a mutual exchange of its components. Clearing up conceptual confusions, removing the tendency or desire to 'criticise a form of life', reveals a distinctive approach to philosophy based on the belief that a state of equilibrium is both necessary and desirable.

Despite all the confusions that have been clarified, all the concepts that have been returned to their appropriate language games, men are still puzzled over the nature of the good life, whether the soul is immortal, whether human freedom is attainable, the nature of God, truth and so on. Despite the entire output of Wittgenstein's successors not one philosophical problem has been laid to rest. Moreover the same questions keep re-appearing. 'Philosophy might be language on holiday but it always goes to the same place'.[22] If contemporary philosophers find its questions unimportant then others who find them important may take it upon themselves to answer them and in so doing define themselves as genuine philosophers. In fact the trivialisation of philosophy, by philosophers, has left the field open for the wild speculations of the pop-ethologists, mystics, charlatans and television journalists, to pass virtually unchallenged in our epoch.

The persistence of certain familiar questions, and the urge to answer them, is demonstrated throughout the *Phenomenology*. According to Hegel they constitute an important feature of any 'form of life'. In fact they are just as essential as the need for consistency in the employment of language and stem from a similar origin. Philosophy will cease to have any meaning when human history ceases, since puzzlement and wonder at the world is an essential characteristic of human beings. Hegel maintains that the activity of philosophy is essential to any form of life that has advanced beyond the level of sense-certainty. The only real physicists he says, are the animals. Philosophy ceases; not because the philosopher has been killed, psycho-analysed, agrees not to upset the public, or because his attention has been diverted to more useful tasks, but when his thirst for knowledge is perfectly quenched, when human history has come to an end.

124

4. THE REALITY OF PHILOSOPHY

> Only among the working-class does the German aptitude for
> theory remain unimpaired. Here it cannot be exterminated.
> Here there is no concern for careers, for profit-making, or
> for gracious patronage from above. [F. Engels, *Ludwig Feuerbach
> and the End of Classical German Philosophy*]

Referring to Aristotle's claim that 'man first begins to philosophise
when the necessities of life are supplied' Hegel adds that insofar as
human beings enjoy the barest level of intellectual sophistication,
philosophy is not a luxury but a necessity.

> Philosophy may be thus called a kind of luxury insofar as
> luxury signifies those enjoyments and pursuits which do not
> belong to external necessity as such. Philosophy in this
> respect seems more capable of being dispensed with than any-
> thing else; but that depends on what is called indispensible.
> From the point of view of Mind, philosophy may even be said
> to be that which is most essential. (GP.MM.70/H.51)

Insofar as there is human language - and this entails a system of knowledge - philosophy will be an essential activity, an essential ingredient
of any system of knowledge, which is why the absolute is to be found in
every shape of consciousness. To be sure, when isolated from each
system of knowledge the content of philosophy is vacuous, but as an
essential aspect of human knowledge its content is truly genuine.

There is a parallel between the relationship, on the one hand, between sense experience and language and philosophy and social existence
on the other. Similarities can therefore be observed between Wittgenstein's account of language and Hegel's account of philosophical discourse. Just as Wittgenstein argued (see Chapter 1) that sense-experience does not have priority over language so Hegel argues that philosophical discourse does not stand in any causal relationship with social
life. Neither philosophy nor sense-experience can be abstracted away
from the wider system of human relationships on which they depend for
their meaning. Commenting on the famous passage in the *Philosophy of
Right* where Hegel says that 'Philosophy is its own time apprehended in
thought', Avineri discerns an element of critical theory in Hegel. 'If
philosophy is then nothing else than its own time apprehended in thought',
says Avineri, 'then there is a curious corollary to it: if a philosopher can only comprehend that which is, then the very fact that he has
comprehended his historical actuality is evidence that a form of life
has already grown old, since only the fully developed can be philosophically comprehended. Thus below the surface of the apparent passivity of Hegel's statement, a basically critical theory can be discerned

...Philosophy is the wisdom of ripeness, and whenever a period in history finds its great philosopher who translates into the language of ideas the quintessence of its actual life, then a period in history has come to a close'.[23] The philosopher's description does not initiate change, it presents the reality of change to those who have not seen it, recording the fulness of the blossom at the moment it is transcended by the flower. On the other hand the universality of philosophy, like the universality of language, suggests that the epoch cannot determine philosophy any more than the objects of sense determine the structure of language. The social order provides no more a foundation for philosophy than philosophy as *nachdenken* provides the foundations for the new social order. According to Hegel the externality of the relationship between philosophy and its epoch, or language and reality, is due to a mistaken tendency to regard them as finite opposites. Such a view is found in S. Rosen's commentary on Hegel's concept of the unity of thought and the world. 'How', asks Rosen, 'can there be a conceptual recollection of a manifestation of the Absolute, if that manifestation is itself a *consequence* of its con ceptual recollection? In sum, *Hegel claims that the actual is brought into being by discourse which can only occur after the actual presents itself*. So far as I can see this is a contradiction *which has no Aufhebung*'.[24] It is only a contradiction if we see the relationship between discourse and the actual as external opposites. Just as neither language nor the objects of sense have finite independence, so with philosophy and its object: it is not a question of whether philo phy precedes the actual or the actual philosophy. Philosophy is given with the actual just as the world is given with language. When Hegel speaks of philosophy arriving 'after a form of life has grown old' in the Preface to the *Philosophy of Right,* the 'after' does not refer strictly to duration but to the impossibility of achieving a separation between philosophy and its epoch, or discourse for the actual. Philosophy as *nachdenken* resembles the relationship between language and the world. Neither language nor philosophy are to be understood as optional extras, as a wall-paper tacked on to the world. Instead they are integrated into the very essence of the world and what the world means to the human beings that inhabited it.

The problem for Hegel is not whether or not metaphysics, but which metaphysic? To engage in any system of knowledge is to embrace certai metaphysical assumptions. Empiricism and logical positivism were neve really alternatives because they too were metaphysical. No matter how hard metaphysics is thrown out it never really disappears. The philosopher who seeks to consign metaphysics to the flames is like the clow who tries to rid himself of a piece of sticky paper; he removes it fro one hand only to find it on the other hand. The more he tries to extricate himself the more he gets tied up in it. It was this kind of reasoning that lay behind one of Hegel's comments on Newtonian physics it was not that Newton had slipped in some occasional metaphysical assumptions, which could be pointed out and eradicated, but that his avowedly anti-metaphysical science was metaphysical, and that precisely because Newton was committed to an anti-metaphysical standpoint he was unable to distinguish the dubious metaphysical assumptions from the more fluid concepts actually necessary for the practice of science.

> Newton gave physics an express warning to beware of metaphysics, it is true; but, to his honour be it said, he did not by any means obey his own warning. The only mere physicists are the animals: they alone do not think, while man is a thinking being and a born metaphysician. The real question is not whether we shall apply metaphysics, but whether our metaphysics are of the right kind: in other words, whether we are not, instead of the concrete logical idea, adopting one sided form of thought, rigidly fixed by understanding, and making these the basis of our theoretical as well as our practical work. (Enz.1.138)

In answer to the charge that philosophy cannot be a genuine activity, since it feeds off genuine activities, Hegel would argue that philosophical puzzlement is as genuine as any other form of human experience. Questions about the soul, freedom, God, life, and so on, express genuine problems that permeate the various branches of knowledge at all levels. They are not confined to the errors perpetuated by an elite of philosophers, whose 'confusions' arise and are dispelled within the university cloisters. Philosophical problems are far from being pseudo problems, as members of the Belgrade Faculty discovered in the early 1970's. Philosophy has deeply affected the lives of generations of men and women and its problems are not created exclusively by a group of specialists indifferent to real problems, whose life-style as well as their language was spent on holiday, such as Wittgenstein's immediate contemporaries who might have genuinely needed to have been led back to the ways of ordinary life. The charge that Wittgenstein's philosophy reflects the separation of academic life from the rest of the culture has been forcibly made by F. Rossi-Landi. Drawing attention to the absence of any theory, in Wittgenstein, to explain why language 'goes on holiday' Rossi-Landi says:

> Wittgenstein's philosophy itself, critical of tradition to the point of sterilising itself by rejecting any theoretical construction which cannot make room for a particular aspect, remains a philosophy in part cut off from reality. In spite of the exasperating fragmentariness, the humble bearing and everyday language, this still reflects the separation of academic life from the rest of culture, of philosophy from the rest of intellectual work, of the society of Oxford and Cambridge from the rest of British culture, and lastly of British society

between the two wars from the rest of the world. The surroundings in which Wittgenstein's fastidious lectures were at home is even that of a group of specialists indifferent to real problems. It is only an idiom spoken mainly by those who have read abstruse books and who belong to a particular clique that language goes on holiday and turns idly *in the way* Wittgenstein typically analysed. He continually said 'we say that...' 'we tend to...' 'we don't take account of...' etc. That no one put him to difficulty by asking to whom this 'we' referred can be explained only on the basis of all these separations the tacit acceptance of which allowed him to assimilate the 'we' to 'all men', which on the contrary is lacking. The naturalness with which the English experience their language (in which after all Wittgenstein taught and conversed) and the connected lack of consciousness of linguistic relativity has certainly contributed to this.[25]

English philosophy during the inter-war years was that of an aristocratic elite, conducted in isolation from the real world. The years of the Wittgensteinian revolution at Cambridge were the years of the depression, Stalinism and the emergence of fascism. Fundamental issues concerning human freedom and existence were raised, discussed and acted upon by millions of men and women the world over. But when we hear of Wittgenstein's agonising sessions at his five to seven discussion class at Trinity on Fridays, none of those present in that hand-picked somnambulant audience recall any of those issues. In the numerous personal recollections of the master during this period one detects an element of frivolity. Karl Britton recalls how 'some who came to it (Wittgenstein's class) after a long afternoon in the open air would be found fast asleep', adding that he often came away with the impression 'that a tremendous effort had been made and little if anything achieved'.[26] What is really significant in Wittgenstein, although he never revealed any awareness of it and it is constantly blurred by the narrowness of his disciples, is the importance given to the expressions and judgments of ordinary people. (Not Moore's abstracted ordinary people, who never held the beliefs of his narrow circle, but real people involved in the daily struggle to transform the world.) There is, on Wittgenstein's terms, no possibility of a criterion for the establishment of a superior standard of discourse and knowledge, no ultimate standpoint which gives one, trained in the use of philosophical terminology, any claim on the title 'philosopher king'. The importance of this can be appreciated once we consider that in the English-speaking world, social divisions have been characterised by linguistic distinctions. But in an age characterised by demands for self-management a reliance upon an elite endowed with a superior linguistic medium decreases in inverse ratio to the confident expression of self-management. Harold Rosen's excellent text, *Language and Class: A critical Look at the Theories of Basil Bernstein,* could well have been cast in Wittgenstein's mould.

Rosen's target is Bernstein's distinction between the 'restricted code' of working class linguistic practices and the 'elaborate' code allegedly employed by the middle classes. Rosen's conclusion is worth quoting at length for it conveys an important message to philosophers of language who have become as equally bewitched by their medium - the English language of Oxbridge and middle-class propriety - as their positivist predecessors were with the language of the exact sciences.

Working-class speech has its own strength which the normal linguistic terminology has not been able to catch. There is no sharp dividing line between it and any other kind of speech, but infinite variations in the deployment of the resources of language. I do not think there are aspects of language usually acquired through education which, given favourable circumstances, give access to more powerful ways of thinking; but given the conditions of life of many strata of the middle-class, the language acquired through education can conceal deserts of ignorance. Moreover the middle-class often have to pay a price for the acquisition of certain kinds of transactional language, and that is a loss of vitality and expressiveness, and obsession with proprieties.[27]

Generally speaking English philosophers have abandoned the search for an underlying logical structure of language only to kneel before the altar of clarity which, in reality, rests paradigmatically on the affections of a middle-class form of social life reflected in its concern for grammatical propriety. Though steeped in Wittgenstein's advice to look at ordinary usage, none of his disciples have listened attentively to cockney, Glaswegian or Liverpudlian linguistic practices and the richness of the cultures reflected by them. But, like the language of the American negroes their deviation from middle-class propriety represents an important area of vitality too often ignored by those obsessed with the standards of correct linguistic formulation.

The language of philosophy is not confined to the discourse employed within the cloisters of professional philosophy. Its problems are universal and unaffected by differences in linguistic style. Philosophical scepticism, a problem to which the later Wittgenstein devoted much effort, has its roots in the lies and distortions of politicians and the media; the problem of other minds has its origins in modern man's inability to communicate, his alienation from his species. The shadow of the concentration camps raises serious problems concerning human freedom and recent developments in genetic engineering, and the employment of life-support systems, raise fundamental questions about the nature of life. To trivialise philosophy, to treat it as a specialist activity or to denounce it as unreal, is to ignore vast dimensions of human experience. If, for instance, we took seriously the thesis that philosophy, being either trivial or specialist, could be dispensed with by the majority of men, we would have to imagine a society in which there would be no grounds for sceptical doubt, where everything would be absolutely clear, where language would have no ambiguity and life would hold no mystery. In the absence of the perfectly-sterilised society we need not fear that philosophy is likely to wither away, nor become a specialist activity, since human institutions themselves reflect both the problems and solutions.

NOTES

[1] See W. H. Walsh, *Metaphysics,* London: Hutchinson, 1963, pp.122-132

[2] See S. M. Easton *The Problem of Knowledge from Marx to Wittgenstein: A study in Idealism*, Doctoral thesis, University of Southampton, 1977; 'Facts, Values and Marxism', *Studies in Soviet Thought,* 1977. A. R. Manser, *The End of Philosophy: Marx and Wittgenstein*, University of Southampton, 1973.

[3] P. Winch, 'Authority' in *Political Philosophy* edited by Anthony Quinton, Oxford: University Press, 1967. pp.96-111.

[4] 'All Characteristically human activities involve a reference to an *established* way of doing things. The idea of such an established way of doing things in its turn presupposes that the practices and pronouncements of a certain group of people shall be authoritative in connection with the activity in question.' Ibid. p.100.

[5] Ibid. p.106.

[6] Lucien Goldmann, *Power and Humanism*, Nottingham: Spokesman, 1974. p.48.

[7] Maurice Brinton's distinction between 'worker's management' and 'worker's control' can throw considerable light on the recuperative effects of the assimilation of *autogestion* to worker's control. Says Brinton: 'In the British movement (and to a lesser extent in the English language) a clear-cut distinction is seldom made between 'control' and 'management', functions which may occasionally overlap but are usually quite distinct. In French, Spanish or Russian political literature two separate terms (*'controle'* and *'gestion'*, *'control'* and *'gerencia'*, *'kontrolia'* and *'upravleniye'*) refer respectively to partial or total domination of the producers over the production process...
...There are words to describe these two states of affairs. *To manage* is to initiate the decisions oneself, as a sovereign

person or collectively, in full knowledge of the relevant facts. *To control* is to supervise, inspect or check decisions initiated by others. 'Control' implies a limitation of sovereignty or, at best, a state of duality of power, wherein some people determine the objectives while others see that the appropriate means are used to achieve them'. M. Brinton, *The Bolsheviks and Workers Control*, Solidarity, 1970. p.ii.

[8] D. Z. Phillips,*Faith and Philosophical Enquiry*, London: Routledge, 1970. pp.237. The quotation is from Kierkegaard's *Fear and Trembling* (1843). For a reply to this view we must go back some forty five years to Kant, who said: 'Abraham would have had to answer this supposedly divine voice: "That I ought not to kill my good son, this is wholly certain; but that you who appear to me, are God, of that I am not certain and never can become certain even if it should resound from the visible heavens"'. From 'The Quarrel Among the Faculties', quoted by W. Kaufmann in *Hegel: A Reinterpretation, Texts and Commentary*, p.271.

[9] J. Loewenberg, *Hegel's Phenomenology: Dialogues on the Life of Mind*, Illinois: Open Court, 1965. p.93.

[10] K. Marx, *The German Ideology*, Part I, edited with an Introduction by C. Arthur, London: Lawrence & Wishart, 1970. p.61.

[11] K. Marx, 'Economic and Philosophical Manuscripts' in *Karl Marx: Early Texts*, translated and edited by D. McLellan, Oxford: Blackwell, 1972. p.133.

[12] Ibid. p.133.

[13] Ibid. p.133.

[14] P. F. Strawson, *Freedom and Resentment and Other Essays*, London, Methuen, 1974, p.116.

[15] R. Rhees, *Discussions of Wittgenstein*, p.46.

[16] G. J. Warnock, *English Philosophy Since 1900*, Oxford: University Press, 1969. p.172.

[17] Ibid. p.166

[18] See Jonathan Ree 'Professional Philosophers', *Radical Philosophy* 1, January 1972, where it is argued that one of the functions of Oxford philosophy is 'its role in preparing an educated ruling class'. pp.2-4.

[19] See *The Attack on Higher Education, Marxist and Radical Penetration,* J. Gould, London: Institute for the Study of Conflict, 1978.

[20] J. P. Sartre, 'Departure and Return' in *Literary and Philosophical Essays,* translated by Annette Michelson, ed. J. L. Hevesi, London: Allan Wingate, 1947. p.139. For a discussion of Sartre's criticism of Parain's theory of language see A. R. Manser, *Sartre: A Philosophical Study,* London: Athlone, 1967. pp.102-3.

[21] See Wittgenstein PI.11, 23, 43, 421.

[22] See A. R. Manser, *The End of Philosophy: Marx and Wittgenstein;* 'If such thoughts are the result of "Language going on holiday", it is surely surprising that it should always spend its vacations in the same place'. p.8.

[23] S. Avineri, *Hegel's Theory of the Modern State,* Cambridge: University Press, 1972. p.128.

[24] Stanley Rosen, *G. W. F. Hegel: An Introduction to the Science of Wisdom,* London, 1974. p.273.

[25] F. Rossi Landi, 'Per un uso Marxiano di Wittgenstein' in *Nouvi Argumenti,* N.S.I., Gennaio, Mar 20. 1966. pp.181-230. This quotation is taken from an unpublished translation by A. R. Manser, University of Southampton.

[26] Karl Britton, 'Portrait of a Philosopher' in *Wittgenstein: the Man and his Philosophy,* edited by K. T. Fann, New York: Dell, 1967. p.56.

[27] Harold Rosen, *Language and Class: A Critical Look at the Theories of Basil Bernstein,* Bristol: Falling Wall Press, 1972. p.19.

Index

Abraham 108-110, 131
Absolute 1, 71, 74, 75, 83, 84,
    87, 88-92, 93, 98, 99, 100,
    103, 108, 123, 125, 126
Anatomy 100
Aristotle 50, 125
Astronomy 98, 99.
Augustine St. 9, 99, 105
Authority 106
Autogestion 107, 128, 130
Avineri S. 125, 132
Ayer A. J. 25

Bambrough R. 80, 81, 102
Bradley F. H. 67, 91, 117
Brinton M. 130, 131
British Labour Party 107
Britton K. 132
Bud and blossom 82, 105, 126
Builders-Wittgenstein's 36, 37,
    38, 43, 44, 45
Burke E. 106, 107, 108

Calculating 17
Cantor Eddie 20-1
Christ J. 106
Civil Society 113
Classification 70
Clark M. 84, 85, 102
Colonialism 33, 109, 113
Commonsense 48, 54, 61, 67, 116
Concrete universal 25
Conservatism 106, 108, 123, 124;
    dynamic conservatism 22, 23
Copernican revolution 63
Crusoe Robinson 29
Cunning of reason 87

Descartes R. 79, 118
Dialectic 57, 69, 90, 94, 111,
    113
Duck-Rabbit 52, 53, 58, 59, 61,
    62
Dummett M. 12

Easton S. M. 130
Eliot T. S. 88
Engels F. 106, 125
Epictetus 112
Facts 11, 13, 14, 15, 16, 17,
    24, 26, 27, 46-53, 82, 92,
    107
Fascism 128
Fear and service 40, 45
Ferre F. 14, 15, 27
Feyerabend P. K. 46, 50, 51, 72
Force and Understanding 68
Forms of life 24, 25, 30, 35-44,
    115, 124
Freedom 111, 112, 128

Gadamer H. 73
Galileo 50, 51
Geach P. T. 55, 72
Gestalt 52, 62, 64
Giving and taking orders 40-42,
    121
God 80, 106, 110, 124, 127, 131
Goldmann L. 107, 130
Good 77, 92
Gould J. 132. Gould Report 118
Grammar 1, 7-11, 13, 26, 48, 49,
    64, 66, 120
Habermas J. 104
Hanson N. R. 48, 52, 71, 72
Hartnack J. 25
Having a point 15, 17-24, 63
Hitler A. 119
Homer 81
Hume D. 101
Hunter J. F. M. 36-40, 42, 44
Hyppolite 103

Idealism 79, 86. Subjective 29,
    53
Identity 6
Illusion 51, 92
James W. 57

Kant I. Int. 74, 101, 121, 131
Kaufmann W. 94, 95, 97, 104, 131
Kepler 51
Kierkegaard S. 78, 102, 109,
   110, 131
Kojève A. 83, 84, 85, 86, 102
Kuhn T. S. 46, 62, 63, 72, 76,
   87, 102, 103

Language games 2, 7, 12, 14, 15
   17, 18, 22, 24, 29, 35, 80,
   106, 108, 109
Lavoisier 63
Lenin V. I. 113
Lewis C. I. 12, 26
Limits of language 87
Loewenberg J. 111, 131
MacIntyre A. 71, 73
McTaggart J. M. E. 90, 91, 103,
   104
Manser A. R. 26, 88-9, 103, 130,
   132
Marcus Aurelius 111
Marx K. 45, 93, 103, 106, 107,
   112, 113, 114, 131
Master and servant 40, 45, 111
Means and ends 91, 92, 99, 100,
   101
Mediate and immediate 49, 50,
   54, 81
Metaphysics 67, 81, 100, 121,
   123, 124, 126, 127
Mill J. S. 117
Moore G. E. 27, 28, 46, 48, 67,
   117, 128
Mormon religion 109
Müller G. E. 93, 96, 97, 104,
   105
Murray D. 73

Names 1, 2, 5
Napoleon 83
Nationalization 107
Nature - uniformity of 70-1
Newton I. 69, 80, 126, 127

Objects 1, 2, 4, 7-9, 11, 29, 31,
   54-58, 61, 64-7, 69, 91, 92,
   93, 98, 100

Over-production 113
Owl of Minerva 83, 85

Paradigm 62, 63, 64, 76
Parain Brice 121
Phenomenological method 3, 43, 44,
   53, 64, 69, 92, 93, 97, 101, 11ĭ
   113, 114, 115, 122
Philosophy - as a competition 76-9
   81, 100, 105; criticism of 102,
   115, 123. Must be descriptive 43
   75, 93, 97, 106, 109, 111, 113,
   114, 115, 126. Futility of 77-78
   Idleness of 120-121. Professiona
   lisation of 115-119. Satisfac-
   tion to its problems 92, 123.
   Reality of 124-130. Revolutions
   in. Int. 76, 79, 81, 128. Sick-
   ness of 93, 117, 121. As trivial
   116-119, 122, 124, 127, 129, 130
   Truth of 77, 78, 79, 81, 82, 97,
   98, 100, 115, 124. Usefulness of
   120-4
Phillips D. Z. 108, 109, 131
Pitcher G. 101, 105
Plant R. Int.
Plato 21, 69, 74, 82
Pöggeler O. 94, 104
Pointing 29, 30, 31
Polygamy 109
Positivism 115, 126, 129
Priestley 63
Properties 54, 55, 56, 57, 58, 64,
   65, 66, 69
Psycho-analysis 123, 124

Racism 33
Ree J. 131
Relativism 62, 72, 77, 101, 109,
   123
Revolution - Copernican 63.
   Philosophical Int.76, 79, 81,
   128. Political 106, 107, 108.
   Scientific 63, 76, 87
Rhees R. 20, 25, 27, 37, 38, 44,
   45, 101, 105, 115, 131
Rosen H. 128, 129, 132
Rosen S. 126-132
Rossi-Landi F. 127, 132

Rules 5, 6, 16, 17, 31, 32, 106
Russell B. 3, 5, 25, 26, 46,
    47, 55, 77, 90, 103, 117

Sacrifice 108, 109, 110
Santayana G. Int.
Sartre J. P. 26, 33, 44, 121,
    132
Scepticism 47, 51, 77, 78, 79,
    81, 129
Schopenhauer A. Int.
Schon D. 22, 28
Seeing connexions 86
Seeing under an aspect 51, 52,
    53, 59, 60
Self-deceit 112
Shakespeare W. 80
Shapes of consciousness 62, 63,
    69, 72, 75, 76, 80, 83, 87,
    93, 94, 96, 97, 102, 106, 111,
    114, 122, 123, 125
Simpson G. G. 4, 25
Smuts Marshall 6
Socialist 107
Socrates 118, 123
Solipsism 3, 29, 53, 54, 69
Soll I. 87, 103
Sophists 118
South Africa 119
Specht E. K. 7, 8, 11, 17, 18,
    26, 27
Spirit 71, 80, 82, 86
Spontaneity 12, 13, 18, 22, 23
Stalinism 119, 128
Standing Bear 26
Stocks J. L. 91, 103
Stoicism 111-3
Strawson P. F. 72, 115, 131
Stroud B. 19, 27
System 24, 25, 28, 29, 74, 85,
    86, 88, 94, 95

Taking seriously 24, 53, 54, 64,
    112, 113, 114, 115, 130
Taylor C. Int.
Taxonomy 98
Thales 90
Theoretical load 48, 51
Tradition 106, 107, 108

Unhappy Consciousness 94, 96
Unofficial strikes 48
Walsh W. H. 106, 130
Warnock, G. J. 116, 131
Webb-Ellis W. 13
Wells H. G. 16
Winch P. 6, 26, 106, 130
Woodsellers 19-20, 22
Worker's control 107, 130, 131
Wyndham J. 73